Nobody Gets Out Of This Alive

More Messages from Our
Loved Ones in the Spirit World

PRISCILLA A. KERESEY

LIVE & LEARN
New York

Published By
Live & Learn
P.O. Box 226
Putnam Valley, NY 10579

Orders: www.liveandlearnguides.com

ISBN: 978-0-9863536-0-4

Printed in the United States of America

For Mum

ACKNOWLEDGMENTS

Many thanks to my clients for the privilege of eavesdropping on the messages from their loved ones in the spirit world, and to the spirit people for sharing their wisdom. Thanks to my mother for offering the benefit of her years as an English teacher; your editing made my writing so much better.

*"I think of death as some delightful journey that I shall take
when all my tasks are done."*
Ella Wheeler Wilcox

TABLE OF CONTENTS

AUTHOR'S NOTE

I wrote my first book *It Will All Make Sense When You're Dead* because 1) the spirit people and my spirit guides were insisting I share their stories; 2) I wanted to dispel the myth that only specially-gifted men and women could talk to their loved ones in the afterlife; and 3) I wanted to show people how to develop their own abilities.

I wrote *Nobody Gets Out Of This Alive* because many of my clients and students asked similar questions about a number of common themes. The spirit people are able to concisely express guidance on difficult subjects such as suicide, forgiveness, and relationships, and their guidance answers those questions with more authority than I could ever provide.

While the spirit people hold forth on many topics, their guidance all seems to boil down to one basic suggestion: that we suspend judgment of ourselves and others.

You'll encounter the term "message circle" throughout the book. I use this to describe what used to be called a séance, a sitting where I act as the medium for a group of three or more guests. I use the words "spirit person" to describe someone who has passed away. You'll also see terms such as "bring in" and "come through," which is how I describe spirit people who present themselves in individual readings or message circles.

As with my first book, all the examples quoted within are taken from actual readings that I personally facilitated in either one-on-one sessions or in message circle groups. All names have been changed to protect identity and privacy.

INTRODUCTION

I'm sitting in my living room with a married couple, and our reading is going along nicely. As a person who is primarily clairsentient and clairvoyant, I get impressions from spirit people as a sense of feeling and a sense of seeing, and today I'm easily feeling and seeing my clients' loved ones. In many respects, this reading is normal and enjoyable, with husband and wife happily validating the details I'm conveying.

So it's with a continued sense of ease that I translate for them what I see next. Our conversation goes like this:

"I see a cherry tree. Do you have one?"

"No," they both say together.

"Hmm. Do you have cherries or like cherries? Did you just make a cherry pie?"

"No," is the response again.

"I know it sounds as though I'm fishing here, but this guy keeps showing me a cherry tree." The image won't go away, so I persist in delivering this message. At times like this, it feels as though I'm trying to hand someone an object that he won't take. The more I insist, the more he resists. Once we get in a cycle of "No," it can be hard to break out of it. It's important for me to help the client stay in a "Yes" frame of mind, because once someone starts shaking her head or saying "No" to me repeatedly, she can effectively shut down her ability to recognize what I'm saying. I have to walk this line cautiously. I'm responsible for translating the image correctly, while also urging the client to look a bit deeper at what I'm saying. When spirit people persist, I know I'm on the right track.

"Really? No cherry tree? There's a male spirit here who keeps showing me this."

"No. No, and no." Now I can tell the wife is getting frustrated.

As I wait a little bit, I ask the spirit man to show me another way to identify him. I want to connect him to his loved ones here, and it's his job to identify himself in a way that will make sense both to me the translator and to this lovely couple on my couch. The man in spirit expands the picture a bit.

"Did you just cut down a tree, a cherry tree or a weeping cherry in your garden?" I try again.

"No," says the husband glancing at his wife, in which gesture I also imagine his eyes are rolling.

Come on, give me something else, I say silently to the spirit. But all he gives me is more of the same. I see him miming to me as if we're in a game of charades, and I'm a total idiot. I see him pointing at the cherry tree, cutting it down, and pointing to himself.

"Did someone cut down a tree?" I ask them. "This spirit is showing himself cutting down a tree." *Am I any good at this at all?* I ask myself.

"I have no idea what you're talking about," the wife says aloud, while I can only imagine what she says to herself.

Good Lord. *What?* I ask the spirit man. He acts out the whole scene again, and it finally dawns on me.

"George is here," I say, understanding at last that the man in spirit is acting like George Washington, arguably the most famous cutter of cherry trees in American history.

"Oh, George! Yes!" the husband crows, welcoming his best friend into our reading.

And that's how a non-clairaudient medium works. Knowing I can't hear them, the spirit people need to show me another way to learn their names. I could see a celebrity, a mythological figure, the face of someone I know, or even an object.

If only the spirit people would routinely use the same famous person for a name, I'd have it much easier. It would be helpful if I could see George Washington cutting down a cherry tree every time a spirit person wanted me to say the name George, but it just doesn't work that way for me. Once a spirit person showed me an image of a character named George Jetson from a 1970s cartoon called "The Jetsons," to prompt me to say the name George. I wonder how silly

I sound going through the same routine: "Do you like the Jetsons? Does that cartoon make sense to you?" and watching the raised eyebrows and head-shaking before I finally realize the spirit wants me to say the name.

One afternoon I was reading for an older woman and a friend she brought along at the last minute. Soon after getting started, I had the impression of a spirit woman whom the friend tentatively identified as her mother. She wanted more evidence, so I asked the spirit for additional impressions.

"Do you drink a lot of coffee?" I asked the friend.

"No," she replied.

"Did you just get a new coffee maker?" I asked.

"No."

"Did something happen with your coffee pot?" I tried again. "She keeps showing me coffee."

"That's our last name," the friend replied. I don't usually take last names when I make appointments, and didn't even know this lady would be coming along. Prompting me to say "coffee" was an easy way for her spirit person to connect to the client and to identify herself.

I recently went to a family home for a message circle, and one of the husbands was visited by his brother in spirit immediately. This brother had died tragically many years ago in young adulthood, and he came into our circle with energy and many clear identifiers. For the next couple of hours other family members happily acknowledged and reminisced with their loved ones in the afterlife, too, and just as we were about to close I turned again to the husband. Throughout the circle I'd repeatedly seen the cover of an old record album by The Charlie Daniels Band. I knew the husband's name was Charlie from our introductions, so I'd resisted mentioning this image. Now it simply grew larger as I tried to dismiss it. Finally I said to him, "Charlie, do you have a Dan or a Daniel in spirit?" Charlie was too moved to respond, but his wife nodded her head and told me, "Dan was his brother's name." The brother in spirit who had been with us for the whole afternoon took the last moments to identify himself by name, using a visual symbol.

My clients and guests like to hear the names of their deceased friends and family to truly believe that their dear ones are near. As a person who relies primarily on a sixth sense of feeling and seeing, hearing names has been a real work-around exercise for me. In asking the spirit people to help me with this, they offer up all sorts of visual images and sensory impressions.

I've been given the messages in this volume the same way. I have not heard them in my mind's ear. The spirit people give me a complex feeling, and then help me translate it correctly. Quite often this translation process takes several minutes as I begin, am corrected by the spirit, and attempt again. For that reason, many of the quotes contain ellipses (...) which serve only to eliminate redundancy or false starts. I've made no other edits.

I wish I could say that the words in this book are mine. They are not. Yes, the words are coming from my mouth and I'm the one translating a feeling into a verbal expression, but I can take no credit for the succinct beauty and wisdom in these messages. Overall, the spirit people encourage us to enjoy our lives with optimism and compassion, and refrain from harsh criticism of self and others. By communicating with us so joyfully, they're inspiring us to embrace the notion that life continues, love survives, and all is forgiven. After all, as the spirit people remind us continually, *nobody gets out of this alive!*

Priscilla A. Keresey
New York, May 8, 2014

PART ONE

"My humanity is bound up in yours
for we can only be human together."
Desmond Tutu

The Human Condition

Spirit people have a great deal to say about their time in the physical body. While we are under no obligation to take their advice, their simple wisdom about healthy living is worth considering. In this section, spirit people touch on what it means to be alive in physical form, the experience of leaving the physical body, and how we might use not only our bodies but our minds to make our time here more comfortable.

Some of the messages you'll read in this section refer to specific diagnoses or medical conditions. Other messages from spirit people suggest specific healing modalities. Please remember that wisdom from beyond is meant to add to our own good judgment, and should never replace medical advice or treatment. Our loved ones in the spirit world recognize that we are controlling our own destinies in part by the use of free will. They also recognize that we are, as they once were, totally responsible for all of our own decisions.

As you read through this section I hope some of these wonderful messages will resonate with you and even inspire you to take good care of yourself physically, mentally, and emotionally. You'll see that it's possible to let go of grief or worry about how your loved one passed, and how you can continue to enjoy life in your own body, with the power of your own mind, in faith, hope, and expectation of reunion in the eternal spirit world.

Our Physical Selves

The Bodies We Die In

"But is she all right?"

Many clients ask me this question, even after an hour with a loved one in spirit who has delivered relevant details and personal messages. Even more are concerned if their loved ones passed suddenly, violently, or far from home. Our cultural beliefs or deep-seated fears about our own demise can lead to a near-obsessive worry about a spirit who left a violently traumatized body, or one whose parts weren't all brought back home to be buried. I've even heard my clients swear they would never become organ donors because of a belief that they wouldn't be able to survive in the spirit world without all or part of their bodies.

My client Nicole's grandmother came through identifying herself by her advanced age, physical appearance, and cause of death. She also emphasized her lady-like demeanor, coiffed hair, fashion sense, and vanity. After Nicole validated her grandmother's presence, this lovely older spirit woman transformed in my mind's eye to about thirty years old. She had a trim waist, dark hair, and lovely skin. Then she made an amazing statement: "Death is the fountain of youth." I was so stunned by this comment I stopped mid-sentence to write it down – even though I was recording the group session. I know what she meant, though this sure was a funny way to say it!

Many spirit people have reported returning to their physical prime once they've gone out to the spirit world. While they don't need bodies exactly, they tell me they are recovering the sense of themselves at their prime. This genteel grandmother appreciated herself best when she looked youthful and trim, and was happy to present herself as enjoying the afterlife this way. She clearly conveyed her meaning in her funny statement: once the physical body falls away, our real immortal selves are ageless. In other words, the physical bodies we exit at death do not define our wholeness in the spirit world.

Spirit people who went to their final resting place without their entire bodies, as well as those who never came home to be buried, present themselves as completely whole. Recently I brought through a man in spirit for one of my guests:

"I have a man coming here who tells me he didn't go to the grave with all of his parts. I sometimes get this feeling when the spirit was an amputee." He showed me a missing arm. "Do you know someone who lost his arm?" I asked, turning to a woman in our group.

"Um... yes!" was her reply.

"Okay, he's here, taking an opportunity to come through and to say, 'I'm whole again.'"

A few moments later I moved on to another guest at the same circle:

"Did you know someone who was injured, no killed, in combat?" I asked.

"No," my guest replied.

"I'm asking because I feel a violent impact to my body. He didn't come home. He shows me the jungle, a terrible impact – as though he hears the sound, no, he *feels* the sound as a concussion. There isn't much left of him. Nothing remains to gather up and bring home. He shows me he was lost and didn't come home. I'm talking about Viet Nam."

"My aunt's fiancé didn't come home from the Viet Nam war but I didn't know him. It was a long time ago," she answered me.

"That's okay," I said. "He's here. He just flashed in to say that even though he didn't come home he's here in the spirit world. No problem that there was no body." My guest was able to confirm that even though she didn't know her aunt's fiancé, she did remember the family's grief that his remains were never brought back to the United States and buried. People often wonder if the spirit person walks the earth unsettled if he isn't brought back home, or if there isn't anything to bury. It's wonderful to hear that this isn't a concern of the spirit people themselves. I continued on:

"Now I'm talking about someone whose body was badly damaged in his passing. I feel a violent explosion – kablam! – a young male."

"A friend of ours died in a [gas] explosion," answered a male guest.

"Okay, he's here too," I said, then took a moment to explain this sequence of visits. "The spirits who have things in common will often come in together, even if they didn't know each other. It's easier for one to ride in on another's details and then add his own. So we have a missing arm, then a violent death in combat, and now, 'while we're on the subject,' we have the next one in the same category." The spirit people have shown me they find it easier to come in through an open door than to cut a new one through to me. If one spirit has shown dying in an explosion (a bomb in combat), he has opened a door that another spirit can come through and with minimal energy shift the details a bit (a gas explosion).

"This man tells me he was alive and then dead. 'I was out,' he says. 'With the impact, I was out.' He wants it to be known that the explosion blew him out. 'I didn't feel it at all.' No discomfort or suffering. A breath blowing him out of the body. He is surprised, but not distressed. He shows me a moment that the accident happened. In this instant there is a whole eternity where he got to see everything. It was instantaneous and eternal at the same time. He had understanding, acceptance, all of these beautiful eternal moments even though it happened in an instant for him. He is peaceful and whole now."

Knowing that our loved ones perish violently, in combat or explosions, can leave us with a more visceral horror than knowing someone we loved died in his sleep. Yet spirit people tell us over and over that *how* they went out of the body is of little consequence to them. They say that dying does not take a long time – declining towards death may, but the act of leaving the body is painless, eye-opening, and simultaneously "instantaneous and eternal."

If you've ever worried that a loved one of yours continues to suffer or roam in limbo because of a lost body or body part, let these messages reassure you. Spirit people repeatedly affirm that the physical body serves us here during physical life, but is of no value to them when they go out to the spirit world.

Spirit people are also indifferent about division or ownership of the deceased's remains. I was asked to do a reading for two sisters in their deceased parents' house. It was winter, and the place was freezing as no one was living in it while it was being prepared for sale. Their mother who had died decades before was the first to come through. Both sisters acknowledged her presence and validated the evidence she presented of her identity. Soon the spirit mother brought in their father, who had passed within the past year. Our reading went along smoothly, and both sisters seemed happy and at peace with their decision to sell their parents' home.

Just as I was about to close, I felt the father grab my attention for one final message.

"He shows me an urn. Usually this means someone was cremated," I said.

"Yes, we had my dad cremated. It's what he wanted," answered one of the sisters, Julia.

"The mother was not cremated," I said. I sensed a problem around the cremation, but I couldn't quite put my finger on it.

"Well, when my dad..." offered Julia.

"No! Don't tell me anything," I interrupted her. "Let *me* tell *you* what the message is. I have a feeling, in this case in particular, that it's important that these words come from your father, and not because of an idea you volunteered." I often have to remind my clients not to give me information. I might allow the client to supplement what I'm bringing through only after she's identified her loved one. It's a natural response for someone to want to fill in or guide what I'm offering, but I feel it could diminish my credibility. For example, if I come to the client with a woman who passed from uterine cancer, that client must be discouraged from responding with, "No, my mother passed from breast cancer." When and if that spirit mother should come through to me, I want the cause of her passing to come from me.

With these sisters I felt the need to interrupt more strongly than usual, and I could tell Julia was startled that I jumped in so forcefully.

"Your dad keeps showing me the urn, and a problem. I'm asking him to tell me, 'Is the problem with his cremation?' No, he shows me a problem with the ashes. Who is Joseph?" I asked.

"That's our brother," answered Megan, the other sister.

"Your father shows me Joseph has a problem with the ashes."

Neither sister said anything as I waited for more.

"He doesn't want to share them because he thinks it's important that every bit of ash stay together in the urn. He doesn't want to spread them or share them with the rest of the family. With you."
Both sisters remained silent, but the tenor of their silence had changed; they were very still.

"Please know that your father is not with his remains anymore. That is not him. If you do not have some of his ashes, it does not mean that you do not have some of *him*. His spirit is completely separate. Don't confuse his spirit presence with the presence of all or part of his physical remains."

When I opened my eyes, both sisters were crying. They acknowledged discord with their brother over this issue. Both were hopeful after our reading that they could repair the relationship with their brother even though he was unwilling to share his father's remains. Julia and Megan also validated the importance of the message coming straight from their father, and not from their suggestion, as they hoped they could share the recording of our reading with Joseph. Hearing straight from his dad that he wasn't attached to the ashes might bring him some peace.

It may be hard to believe the bodies that we're so attached to while here in this life become completely meaningless to us once we leave them. Yet spirit people neither sentimentalize their previous physical form nor seem to have any nostalgic love for it at all. When they come through with these messages, I believe they hope to show us that even though we identified them with their physical bodies, it's important we don't identify them solely *as* those bodies. We might believe if the body is gone, or doesn't come home, or is violently torn apart in death, that the lovely spirit who inhabited it is also gone forever, cannot come home, or is somehow torn apart. The spirits tell us that's simply not so. Of course it makes sense that we become attached to the beautiful eyes of our spouse, or the soft skin of our child, or the strong arms of our dad. It's true that those physical representations of the loved one slip away in death. But the light that shines from those eyes, puts that rosy glow in the child's cheek, and builds that strong muscular body is eternal and cannot be destroyed no matter how violent the passing.

More than one spirit person has even joked about her physical form after passing. If you read my last book *It Will All Make Sense When You're Dead*, you'll remember the story of a girl in spirit who had been hit by a train. Her cousin was among the circle guests I was reading. The young lady showed her cousin making fun of the way the mortician reconstructed her nose for the viewing. The spirit had a great time laughing at her mortified cousin, saying, "I'm lying here in a casket, and all you can talk about is how my nose looks?!"

A spirit person knows that right after passing his loved ones are still looking at the deceased body as though it is he, himself. You wouldn't believe the number of family members who argue over what the deceased would want to wear in the casket. The spirits witness their grief-stricken families bickering over which dress is appropriate, whether he would want to be wearing a tie, whether a child would be more comfortable in pajamas than his Communion suit. One young man told me his mother-in-law hadn't spoken to him in years because he felt his deceased wife, who loved wearing his New York Jets football jersey, would want to wear it to Heaven. His mother-in-law felt her daughter should go before God in her best dress.

In order to diffuse this ongoing tension, regret, or family disharmony, laughing spirit people frequently tease, "I have to spend eternity in *that?*"

As you can see from these various messages, spirit people I've brought through have no attachment to their earthly remains. How or whether their physical form is handled according to custom is immaterial to the spirit which once embodied it. They encourage us to be free of our attachment to the physical form of the loved ones who have passed away, and enjoy the memory of their laughter, love, and energy. Those things can never die. And no matter how they passed, or whatever their final outfit, the consistent answer to the question is, yes, they are all right.

Disconnecting from the Physical Body

Even though the spirit people tell us their exit from the body is instantaneous, sometimes we see a dying process that takes years.

During a message circle, a man in spirit appeared for his son

Michael who was sitting directly across from me. After identifying his father through the many bits of evidence he offered, Michael wondered if his father had a message for him. I hear this question almost every day, yet the truth is not all spirit people have specific messages to deliver. In my experience, many of the spirit people simply want to prove that they are still alive, maintaining relationships with their family and friends in the physical world. Their messages consist of normal, everyday dialogue. Not every connection results in profound, life-altering, karma-clearing, problem-solving messages.

For example, when I was a less-experienced medium I did a phone reading with a client in a different state. As usual, I ask a client not to give me any information about whom she is hoping to connect to. I first shared my awareness of a woman in spirit who had an issue with one of her lower legs from polio. I then mentioned that she passed from emphysema. In addition, the spirit showed me Saint Claire, indicating she had a name resembling Claire or Clarice. She showed me herself above and slightly to the right of the client, which told me she was an aunt on her mother's side. After my client validated those details, the spirit aunt brought in another woman at her side, saying "Sister." I told this to my client and that this second woman was handing her a diamond pin; I concluded her mother had given her this pin, and we now had the presence of her mother in spirit. Once again, my client validated. The mother showed me a bouquet, which for me is a symbol of an anniversary. My phone client told me that the day of our reading was the one-year anniversary of her mother's passing.

We carried on for about an hour, with both mother and aunt in spirit deepening the connection by bringing in other identifying, unique details about their lives or what was happening in my client's life since both had passed. Mother mentioned my client's brother by name, and that she saw him traveling in Texas, where he indeed was at that time. Mother noted daughter's anxiety about finding a job, which was also validated. In other words, what transpired was much like a regular conversation between a mother and daughter who hadn't spoken in a while. At the end of our session, my client asked if her mother had a message for her. For a moment I couldn't think of anything to say. I wanted to say, "Well, yes, you just heard an hour's worth of messages." I hadn't learned yet that what most clients need to hear is that their loved one is okay, or that she didn't suffer, or that she forgives the client for any perceived offense.

I went specifically to the mother in spirit and asked her to help me resolve whatever was unfinished in her daughter's relationship with her. Her mother said, "I saw you trying to help me, and it's okay that I died." My client sighed heavily as if with relief, and told me that she had tried to administer CPR, but her mother died before the paramedics could take over. With that, she was satisfied with our reading, and I wondered to myself if any of the other pretty cool connections had mattered at all. So when a client asks me if his spirit person has a message for him, I've learned that what he he truly wants to know is whether that spirit has an answer to his specific question.

When I tuned back to Michael's father in spirit, I went directly to the same question in my mind: "What can I tell your son so that he resolves any unsettled feelings about your passing?"

After the father's response to me I said, "He appears to be isolated, not able to interact with people around him. He's in a nursing home or hospice. People perceived he was lost or isolated. This is the fog that symbolizes Alzheimer's Disease."

"Yes, my dad got Alzheimer's very young and was in a nursing home before he died," Michael replied.

"You visited often at first but then not so much after he didn't recognize you. He sees that this was painful for you, and he doesn't blame you. He says, 'A young man doesn't want to be around that confusion anyway.'"

My client had a catch in his throat as he validated. "I was only twenty-one years old back then. I loved my dad, but he didn't recognize me and I just couldn't handle it. I said that exactly, 'I'm a young man and I shouldn't have to deal with this stuff.' I was in school and I had a girlfriend and I just couldn't deal with it. I was mad at him. Can you believe that?" He was crying openly now.

"I'm not done with his message," I told him. "He doesn't want you to think that just because you perceived him to be lonely and isolated, that he was in fact lonely and isolated. He gives me a feeling of a bird inside of him, flitting from thought to thought to thought, so internally he is much entertained. He says, 'I couldn't articulate.' He wants me to say that the information came in, he was aware of people interacting with him, but the bird didn't sit still long enough to come down here to the mouth and let a response come out. A tiny bird would go from one memory to another to another; he's not just zoned out. He's watching something play out inside of his mind, and he was quite okay even though he couldn't indicate that he was."

In time, this man passed away without ever recognizing anyone again, but he clearly tells us that this was not nearly as painful for him as it was for his family members. He didn't depart from his physical body until after living with this "bird" for several years. Despite appearances, it wasn't a slow and painful years-long departure. With this message, he released Michael from years of worry that his beloved dad had faded away feeling lonely and isolated, as though his spirit were slowly being extinguished as his physical capabilities diminished.

***

Two women asked for someone who hadn't yet come forward with the other spirit people during the first forty-five minutes of our hour-long reading. They were anxious to hear from Warren, so I went looking for him. At times like these, I ask my clients to validate anyone who comes through, because if I do not connect directly to the one they're looking for, an intermediary spirit may act as medium in the afterlife.

When I go looking, I'm simply asking all the other spirit people for silence as I seek out any thought, feeling, picture, sound, or twinge in my sixth sense. In the midst of this search for Warren, I felt as though I were thrown against a hard surface.

"I'm not connecting with Warren yet, because this spirit is a young woman. I feel a violent trauma. Was there a hit-and-run? Can you make a connection to this? It sounds funny, but I'm seeing hit *with* a car and hit *by* a car at the same time."

"No," they both said.

"I have someone here who gives me the feeling of my chest exploding. This is a vehicle accident. I have violent trauma in the front of my body, and then I'm tumbling around on the road. Do you know who I'm talking about?"

"It's a male?" One client offered to acknowledge a male who was hit by a motorcycle.

"No, not this one," I replied. "This is a young woman, and it's a car, not a bike."

"Oh! My friend went through the windshield then into the road and got run over," said one of the women.

"This is who I'm talking about. This is ugly, violent," I said.

"I was just talking to her mother this morning. They didn't even want to tell anyone, it was so awful," was the reply.

"I'm not connecting with Warren yet, but let me get this person through. Was there a mystery about how this happened?"

"Yes. She was alone."

"Okay, that's why I got the hit-and-run feeling. Because I feel, 'How did this happen?' then violent destruction of the body," I said. "She shows me reaching [towards the passenger seat floor]. When her body turned, she involuntarily turned the steering wheel. That's the feeling that she gave me. There's a sense of a distraction. And then, bang. Horrible."

"She was asleep," my client said.

"No, she wasn't asleep," I said.

"They were saying she was asleep, then someone people thought maybe she was drunk, or someone cut her off, or an animal could have," my client said. "They just don't really know."

"No," I said. "I get a definite feeling when someone is drunk, and this girl is not drunk."

"Yeah, we didn't believe that either," said both women.

"She shows me reaching down and over, and the hand goes a little and the car turns a little, right off the road. She does not give me the feeling of being drunk."

"We all said that, too," her friend said. "We were told she fell asleep at the wheel."

"The car went to the right and hit the guardrail," I said. "Please tell her family —"

"I was just talking to her mother in Florida, and she was asking about you," my client interrupted. Apparently this young woman's mother knew her friends would be visiting a medium.

"Well, I'm glad she came through. Please say that her daughter was not drunk. It was a distraction, nothing else," I said.

"Her mother writes to me all the time," said my client.

"Her daughter wants to clear her name. It was her actions, but it wasn't because she made a bad decision. She shows me, 'I'm alive, then dead.' You know how we say, 'She didn't know what hit her'? She didn't know what hit her. I'm reaching, and then I'm in the spirit world. Surprise, but no fear. I see no negative reaction. She gives me a feeling of a vapor released from a jar. Just spreading out and aquiring a multi-dimensional awareness. As though she were a gas in a jar that comes out and goes in all directions, taking up more space. Every point of her becomes a feeling point. I never heard this before; it's beautiful." This was such a difficult sensation to describe, that I kept trying to convey it accurately.

"She says when she was alive, she had a central point of consciousness. As though her sense of Self were located in one place in her person. I don't even know how to say this. When she passed, her sense of one, local Self instantly changed. Again she shows me something similar to a vapor being released from a jar. That one Self spreads out and every particle of the vapor also becomes a point of consciousness. One sense of Self becomes many. She gives me the sense of being huge in an instant, and knowing, understanding, and loving everything. Her well-being is emanating from this vapor that escapes the personhood of her body. Even her passing wasn't traumatic for her, I think that's what she's trying to say. Obviously it's traumatic for everyone she left behind, but she shows me an instant of being alive, and then being alive in a wholly, totally different way. And seamless. Surprised, but super-aware."

Trying to articulate that feeling had me stumbling on for another several minutes, but it was worth it. This young woman left her body in an instant. She never saw it coming. Her disconnect from her body was a pinpoint moment in time, just as it had been for Michael's dad who spent years with a terminal brain illness called Alzheimer's Disease. In her case, the body shut down instantaneously rather than taking years. In both cases the spirits themselves exited in a fraction of a second, whole and vibrant. Not diminished, but expanded.

After sharing her message, the young spirit woman connected us to Warren. We finished our reading with everyone feeling satisfied.

***

One of the most profound impressions a spirit person ever gave me to translate was the sensation of disconnecting from the physical body for the final time – in other words, dying. This particular woman had fallen down an elevator shaft after leaving an office party, and as the car below dropped away beneath her, suddenly it was as if I myself were plummeting down. I could hear screaming above me. Time passed at a crawl while seeming also to speed up. I remember thinking as I was falling – because I couldn't separate myself from the experience – *If the elevator stops soon I'll hit the top and I'll probably be okay. I'll probably break some bones but I think I'll live.* But the elevator continued to drop far beneath me as I fell faster. Even then I had time to think, *Okay, if the car stops now I'll hit the top of it hard, but there's a chance I'll still live through it.* After another moment, I realized that even if the elevator car were to stop now I would hit it too hard to survive. In fact, I could see that I wasn't falling directly down the center but was coming quite near to one of the sides. Soon I'd glance off one of the horizontal beams that protruded slightly into the shaft, and then it would be all over.

I closed my eyes when I realized the inevitability of this strike. I was certain I was going to die, and I said to myself, *Well. Okay.* Total calm descended as I plummeted down to my death, and I waited for what would surely be a violent impact. But as I waited I felt a soft vibration or ripple throughout my entire body, and I was next aware that I was simply awake and in the world once again.

Though this was a terrifying experience to recount, with the screaming in the background and the thoughtful analysis of injuries I would sustain when and if the car stopped below me and I hit it, the spirit had me recall that during that fall I was supernaturally calm. And when my mind arrived at the obvious conclusion, it was exactly okay. The moment I braced myself for, slamming into a concrete wall, made no impression on my spirit in the least. Dying felt like a slight pleasant shiver before waking up. It was similar to that moment in the morning when you realize you're awake. When your awareness seems to shift from one form to another, bringing with it a sense of being in the here-and-now. The next time you're able to wake up without an alarm clock, try to feel that shift in your self-awareness the moment you understand you are now awake. Even if your eyes aren't yet open, you sense your place in the world that a moment ago wasn't identifiable. The shift is slight. If allowed to surface naturally instead of being jarred awake by an alarm, the mind self-identification is subtle, easy, and pleasant. The woman who fell down the elevator shaft showed me that this is how she experienced dying, though her physical remains were so completely shattered it was hard for witnesses to believe she didn't feel any pain.

***

During a message circle for a family one day, I brought through a man who passed before his time. Spirit people say, "I passed before my time" when they mean they died young. They'll tell me, "I lived to the end of my life" when they passed away at an advanced age.

"He tells me he passed before his time. He gives me a sense of speediness, of altered state of consciousness. He says, 'It wasn't supposed to go this far.' Do you know who I'm talking about? This is a young man who shows me a drug overdose," I said to one of the young women in our group. "He also wants me to talk about the phone."

"Yes!" she said, "that's my friend Ben. We had this stupid joke about a phone, and you wouldn't know that but he would definitely say it. I know it's him!"

"Someone else was with him," I told her. "Someone who felt he should have done something. Ben is taking full responsibility for his actions. It wasn't supposed to go as far as passing away."

"That's right, he wasn't alone when he overdosed."

"He shows me this moment where eternity begins and where he steps into it. This moment is quite beautiful.

"I hear you crying," I said, though I wasn't looking at my guest. When a spirit person is giving me impressions they are either of the feeling sort or the visual sort, and when I have visual impressions I work with my eyes closed. "I hear you crying, but I want you to know

33

he's showing me a beautiful, seamless, easy, fully-aware process where he comes right up to the doorway of life – physical life – and as he's stepping through it he realizes that he's made a mistake, he's overdone it, and he can't go back.

"But he's also tells me, 'Wow!' He shows me an eternal moment of awe. I wish I could give you the feeling he's giving me because I'm thrilled when I see this! Even though he has this awareness of "Oops!" it pales in comparison to this eternal moment that is still going on. And stepping over that threshold he has this understanding [of having just caused his own death] but it doesn't touch him. I don't mean it to sound harsh, but he says it doesn't touch him the way it would touch our human personality with emotion, such as, 'Oh no, my life is over!' He shows me, 'So what?' He has real joy along with the awareness of a mistake he made, and when he realized he wanted to put the brakes on it was too late, but that ended up being okay with him. Obviously it was not okay with those he left behind in such distress, but he wants to convey that he is fine."

"He knows he was dying?" she asked.

"He shows me he knew at a certain moment that he had crossed a line where he wouldn't survive. At the same exact moment, he began to experience another amazing kind of life. A part of him said, 'Oops, that act went too far and I didn't intend to go someplace I couldn't return from,' but at the same time he knew that where he was going was just fantastic."

"Do you have a tattoo?" I asked my guest. "He points to a tattoo on you with a wing, an angel or fairy wing."

"Yes!" she cried.

"We both just want to make sure that you are sure it's Ben," I said.

"Oh, I'm sure. The minute you said that about the phone I knew it was him."

***

In another message circle, I met another spirit who had taken his own life. Unlike Ben in the previous example, this man consciously chose to commit suicide. Spirit people will show me various degrees of ownership in the cause of passing by showing me distinct symbols.

A spirit like Ben will tell me "My actions led to my passing." A spirit who purposely ends his own life will say "I took myself out." Sometimes a spirit will just hold up her hand to indicate that her lifestyle or behavior began a series of events that caused her death. Each one admits responsibility in a different way, depending upon how conscious the choice was and how soon the actions led to dying.

I asked my guest, "Do you know someone who was shot? A young adult male spirit gives me the feeling of a gunshot."

My guest told me she didn't know anyone who died from a gunshot wound.

"This is a man, and he gives me a sense of shooting himself," I clarified. "His passing is fairly recent. This man is someone you know who is just outside your regular circle. He shows me his family circle and yours, and that they only touch a little bit."

"Oh!" my guest cried out as I was describing the circles, "the family next door to our summer house in upstate New York – their twenty-seven year old son shot himself two months ago."

"He's taking this opportunity to come in and explain himself. He did it, but the *choice* to do it was an accident. He shows me between pulling the trigger and being hit with the bullet, he knew it was a mistake. There was a second of awareness, almost like being of two minds. It happened accidentally, but he also did it on purpose."

"I don't get it," she replied. "If I see his parents I want to tell them he came through but I want to make sure I totally understand his message. I don't want to upset them."

"He's acknowledging, 'I shot myself,' but he's also saying, 'a part of my mind knows it was an accident because I didn't mean to, or I didn't want to, or I knew at the last minute after it was too late to take the bullet back, that this was a mistake.' He wants to say this."

"Okay," she said.

"He tells me people were wondering if it was an accident, and he's saying, 'Accident. I did it on purpose, but I knew it was an accident.' He wants to be here, he wants it acknowledged that he's here in the Heavenly world with all of the other wonderful spirit people who did not take their lives. People who killed themselves don't go to a special place in Hell."

"I will definitely tell his folks that!" my guest replied.

"He says, 'We're all here in the spirit world. Nothing's going to happen to me.' I haven't felt or seen this before. He shows me that time stopped. He had an awareness of this fraction of a second between pulling the trigger and being hit by the bullet. A moment of, 'Oh, no.' A tiny little sliver of time stretched into eternity for just a moment, and that's when he had time to think about it. He went through all of this thinking and awareness and understanding, and then time collapsed again, and he's gone. I never had this feeling before, of time stopping and becoming elastic and stretching out. He had this moment that turned into plenty of time to figure things out, and then time continues again and life, for him, ends."

"So he didn't suffer?"

"Oh no!" I said. "How can he suffer when he has this new understanding? He sees his family suffering. He shows me a barn and a car."

"He went to the barn on the property where there was an old car. His parents saw him go out there but nobody knew he was going to kill himself. Now of course they all think they should have known and stopped him, because another family member killed himself a few years before. His family feels they could have prevented it. They're just torturing themselves."

"Please tell them he isn't lost anywhere. He understands the full impact of his actions, but he is absolutely not telling me he is being punished for them. He tells me people aren't punished for learning, and that was a long moment of learning for him. Please tell them he is okay, and they couldn't have prevented it."

We die in all sorts of ways, both drawn out and quick, by accident or our own hand. Yet in every example, the spirit people talk about the moment of death with awe and amazement. The instant the spirit withdraws permanently from the physical body, she experiences what has no equal in our physical world. The spirit people dismiss their passing and the body as now inconsequential. I know this runs counter to many stories we hear about spirits roaming the earth, having to live in limbo, seeking out their killers, or haunting family members who should have "done something." In all the years I have been privileged to pass on messages from the dead, never once have those stories been borne out. I repeatedly hear stories of rebirth and redemption, instant and complete understanding, dropping the old without a second thought, and joyfully embracing the new. If we keep this in mind about our loved ones, no matter how they passed, we can hope to experience healing and peace sooner.

Health Advice From A Spirit To Her Husband

As a psychic medium, my clients' questions center around health, money, and love. I call these The Big Three. Of these, the subject of health is the touchiest. When a client asks me about her own health or the health of a family member, ethically I must tread carefully. When spirit people comment on a client's health, they usually do so because they're making a connection, such as, "You got that from me." Sometimes they'll also use that message to offer a gentle warning to be more proactive than they had been when alive in the physical body.

In a private reading for my client Tamara, her mother came in immediately. After acknowledging several identifying characteristics, and assured that this spirit was indeed her mother, I asked Tamara:

"She shows me mushrooms. Do you cook with mushrooms?"

"Well, I cook with mushrooms, but..." answered Tamara.

I asked the spirit person to let that build up some more, as I admitted to my client that perhaps I didn't get that connection right. When I've made the right connection or translated a message correctly, the spirit gives me a *zing!* feeling that seems to run right up my spine. Tamara's lukewarm response about sometimes cooking with mushrooms didn't give me the *zing!* feeling I was expecting, so I knew I either hadn't translated the image correctly or wasn't going in the right direction. We carried on with her reading, and as we neared the end of the hour, I said, "I want to talk about this mushroom thing again. Who had cancer?"

"My mother did, and my stepfather has it now," Tamara answered.

"Okay, she talks to me about mushrooms and cancer. Did she take a mushroom extract?" I asked.

"I don't know if it was mushrooms. I think it was some sort of Tahitian millweed juice," said Tamara.

She volunteered the second part before I could stop her. Nevertheless I concentrated on Tahitian millweed juice. No *zing!*

"No, this is an actual mushroom she's showing me. I am not a doctor; I am not making any diagnosis or prescription. Her husband has cancer now? She is talking about mushrooms for this. Please ask him to just search 'mushrooms and cancer,' because I have a feeling about an extract or supplement that's made from a special mushroom. An element in a certain mushroom is going to make this process easier, and that is what she wants to say to him." Tamara looked unconvinced, so after reiterating my disclaimer that I was not dispensing medical advice, I said, "I'm going to stop right there."

Whether I'm giving a reading using my psychic ability or spirit communication ability, commenting on issues of a medical nature, including questions about pregnancy and death, requires extreme caution. When I'm tuning in psychically, I'm using my sixth sense to gather information from a physical object about the physical world. For example, when I hold on to someone's watch, look at a photograph, stand in particular location, or even listen to the voice of my client over the phone, I'm using a technique called psychometry. I'm ignoring the input from my five physical senses and concentrating on my sixth sense to receive impressions. The reception of those impressions for me is in the form of feeling (clairsentience) and seeing (clairvoyance). I generally do not get impressions in the form of hearing (clairaudience).

Spirit communication also involves the sixth sense. It's called mediumship and is distinct from psychometry only in that the information comes from a person in the spirit world and not from the physical world. Some mediums may be different, but I receive impressions both psychically and as a medium in the same way, through the impression of feeling and seeing.

In either case, the impressions that come through are subtle and require interpretation to take them from the sixth sense part of my mind, which can feel like the imagination, into the five senses part of the mind, which is rational, logical, and tangible. One way to describe this process is to imagine you're sitting with someone when an old song comes on the radio. Suddenly you're flooded with the memory and the feeling sense of who you were long ago, when you first heard it. Your companion sees you start to smile and asks, "What is it?"

It takes a lot to explain how you're feeling, what you're recalling, and all the things you're re-experiencing. You can't describe it all in one word or a simple phrase. It's just not that easy to translate an emotional, mental, and physical experience. Even though it may have happened thirty years ago, you may feel it as if it is all happening again, right now. That's how a spirit person pushes an impression on me. Not only do I see the image she wants to show me, but I get her emotional and physical feelings as well.

When a client asks me about health issues I tune in to the energy of her body. I say that I'm scanning it, but I'm actually paying attention to feelings in my own body – any twinges, highlights, or pictures. I might feel or see a red circle around my right knee, or feel an ache in my neck. I share what I'm feeling without suggesting to the client what might be the cause. Usually I hear, "Yes, my knee has been bothering me," or "I hurt my neck and I'm going to the chiropractor this afternoon." When clients ask me about future health, I do the same thing pushed a bit farther into the future. The only time I receive impressions about serious health issues is if the information I get can mitigate it some way.

***

Years ago I did a reading for Tina, who owned a local fitness franchise. During our reading, I felt a funny pull in my chest. Tina hadn't asked me to look at her health, but this weird feeling certainly stood out.

"May I talk about health for a minute?" I asked her.

"Okay..." she drawled out.

"I have this bizarre ache on the left side of my chest. Not my breast, behind it. Not my heart. My chest muscle. Did you get a bruise here or pull a muscle?" I prompted.

"No, I don't remember, why?" Tina started to look a little panicky. I concentrated a little harder on this feeling, allowing pictures and other impressions to float into my awareness. The iconic image of the cancer ribbon is an impression that signifies cancer in my readings, and I looked hard for this symbol. I waited a bit more, looking specifically for the ribbon. It was nowhere to be found.

"If you aren't feeling this now and you haven't felt it in the recent past, then I'm going to make a prediction. I feel this hard knot of pain here," I touched my chest right under my left collarbone. "I sense alarm. I feel worried, waiting. But my overall impression is that everything is okay."

"You mean something's going to happen to me? I have cancer?" Tina asked.

"No! That's the good news. My impression is that you will feel a small pain, get it checked, there may be some anxious waiting, but then a huge sense of relief because nothing is wrong. When that happens, do what you need to do but keep your cool. Everything is going to be all right." I continued on with our reading, including my impression of a speeding ticket for her husband.

I didn't see or hear from Tina for several months, but we caught up at the bank one day when we were both waiting in line. She told me she'd felt a lump in her chest and had gone to her doctor. It turned out to be nothing, as predicted, but she laughed when she said her family couldn't believe that she wasn't totally panicked while waiting for the results. I asked her if she remembered our reading, and said, "It was because of our reading that I didn't freak out. You told me my husband would get a speeding ticket, and he did. The other things you told me also came true. So when I found this bump I said to myself, 'If she was right about those others things, she's right about this, too.' And I just didn't panic. It all worked out!"

I share this example because it is only in a context such as this that I will receive impressions about health issues or medical emergencies. A frequent client referred a young woman to me a while ago. During our reading, this new client asked me if she would deliver the baby she was carrying. She'd had several miscarriages after her first child was born, and was feeling worried about the outcome of her current pregnancy. She was teary-eyed and anxious, sitting on the edge of the couch and twisting her tissue into knots. We have a saying in the psychic business: "Don't ask the question if you truly don't want to know the answer," but this is much easier said than done. I could tell that my client wanted badly to know and not know at the same time. I happen to be trained as a clinical hypnotist, having spent more than fifteen years studying and practicing hypnosis, and I'm acutely aware of the tremendous power of suggestion – particularly for a person in a highly emotional state. When a client asks me a question whose outcome I (or she) might influence through suggestion, the responsibility of answering sensitively and cautiously lies entirely with me. If I were to tell her that I see a miscarriage, that might be suggestion enough to cause one. If I were to tell her everything is going to be fine just to prevent further upset, she might ignore physical symptoms that require medical attention.

At times like this, I close my eyes and ask for information that will best serve the client. In a short time, I could clearly see two healthy children playing at her feet, and told her so. She breathed a sigh of relief, and we concluded our reading. I heard through our mutual friend a short time later that she had in fact miscarried, and was upset with me because I told her that she wouldn't. Today she has two healthy daughters, and I have never seen a reason to correct her interpretation of our reading.

These are just two examples of the sensitive nature of health questions, and the balance I am ethically and legally compelled to find between honestly sharing what is coming to me and understanding the powerful suggestions clients might infer from my impressions. Combined with the understanding that I'm simply translating what I feel the spirit person is trying to get me to say, I make sure to repeat my disclaimer several times. When Tamara's mother in spirit was talking about mushrooms for cancer, I had to remind Tamara that neither I nor the spirit person was qualified to give medical advice. I was simply passing on the information. Both of us were a bit skeptical, and I moved on with the reading.

A couple of weeks later I received this email from Tamara:

During my reading two weeks ago, my mother's spirit was showing you an image of a mushroom which we couldn't figure out at first. Later on in the reading, you concluded that it was a message to my stepfather in reference to his having cancer, and that my mother was telling him to find a certain mushroom he could take to help with his illness.

I kept thinking about this mushroom, since it was one of the few things I couldn't make sense of from my reading. I googled "mushrooms" and "cancer," as you told me to, but nothing seemed to stick. I was thinking about shrugging off my search for this cancer-fighting mushroom.

Yesterday, February 8th, would have been my mom's 65th birthday. My stepdad called me last night sounding really urgent about something, so my husband put my phone on speaker so that I could hear what he had to say, even though I was driving. [My stepfather] said his friend had just come over and told him this story, and that I had to hear it as well. His friend came on and told me that when he was at work, one of his co-workers from South Africa, who he didn't usually speak to except in passing, pulled him aside to show me a sort of mushroom he had been taking to prevent cancer, since it runs in his family!

My stepdad's friend visits with my stepdad regularly, so of course he passed on the story about the mushroom when he went to see him after work yesterday. However, he was only passing it on as an option for my stepdad, and he didn't know anything about my reading. My stepdad (a "healthy skeptic") had listened to my recording of the reading though, and he was incredulous! Of course, he told his friend that they had to share this story with me right away, and now he has every intention of buying these mushrooms to use himself!

I wanted to let you know how it seemed that my mom was insistent on getting this message of the mushrooms through, and how we're all amazed by the entire situation!

Our spirit people can offer us their opinions, and psychics can share what they see regarding health, but we still have free will and it's up to us in the physical world to take care of our physical bodies. Tamara's mother had an insight about mushrooms that neither one of us could validate at the moment. How it was the spirit mother happened to know about this treatment is also unanswerable. That's why it is imperative to remember that a psychic or medium often won't know the source of the message. Sometimes we may not even be one hundred percent sure ourselves of the information that comes through. Any psychic or medium who supplies you with impressions about your health should leave you feeling empowered and not helpless or anxious. An ethical medium should remind you that you are not compelled to take a spirit person's advice, and an ethical medium will never offer you counseling herself unless she is a licensed therapist. What the spirit people have to say about physical health or specific treatments or diseases in particular is gathered from their own experience on earth and their perspective in the afterlife.

Perceiving Wellness Instead of Sickness

Pam was sitting with me for a reading when her aunt came in from the spirit world. After I'd offered evidence to identify her, the aunt wanted to talk about Pam's father, who was sick.

"She says, 'Just because we perceive something it doesn't mean that it's real. The only thing that's real is God's holy perfection in every one of us, and if you see that, that's what you will perceive. Try to see your father as God sees him, which is whole and healed and perfect, because illness is a perception. If you perceive illness, it will make your reality, but if you see the reality, which is how God made him, then you will perceive your father as God perceives him, which is healed and whole.' I was a little surprised and confused by this comment from the spirit world, but passed it on nonetheless.

"I don't understand that," Pam said. "I should pretend my father isn't sick?"

"I'm not sure I understand it either," I replied, and silently asked the spirit aunt to clarify her message. "She says, 'Start to look at all that's right and going well, and see that he is healed. Only allow this, though obviously you're going to [take him to his doctors and get him the medical care he needs]. Every night in your prayers say, "Thank you for healing my Dad," instead of "God, please heal my Dad." When you look at him, try to see past the ailment. When you look into his eyes see the healthy Dad.'"

Pam's father-in-law in the spirit world, whom we had identified and greeted earlier in our reading, picked up the thread.

"He shows me the side-view mirror of a car, where he points out, 'Objects in the mirror are closer than they appear.' It looks as though his healing is far off in the future, but it's closer than it appears," I said.

"It's funny he would use that metaphor because yesterday my daughter and I got in the car and the side-view mirror had been nearly twisted off," said Pam.

Spirit people often use recent events to show that they still know what's going on in the day-to-day lives of their physical loved ones, and often take the same event as an opportunity to symbolize a message. This message touched me on many levels, as it so eloquently captures what I know deep down to be the shortcut to all well-being in the world.

The world as each one of us experiences it is unique. The universe I perceive is the world I live in; when I die, that world ends because my human perception of it ends. If I am suspicious and distrustful of others, my experience will reflect that. If I presume goodwill on the part of others, I will enjoy a happy sense of community where neighbors help and look out for each other. My experience as a hypnotist bears out this theory, as well. The expectation of a certain outcome and the repetition of a belief almost guarantee it. For example, I have weighed the same since high school. Why? Because I expect that I will always stay within a certain weight range and because I've repeated it personally as a way to maintain a healthy weight. My friends from home say, "Priscilla, you look just as you did in high school!" and I agree with them. And so it is with my health, my business, my relationships, and my home. What I expect and perceive is what I get.

When I heard this wonderful news from the spirit people, I knew I was on the right track. If you're fighting a health battle, acknowledge the issue and follow the advice of your medical professionals, but also expect that you'll recover. See, imagine, or feel yourself at your best. Tell everyone who asks that you're feeling much better, thank you, and far sooner than you ever thought possible your life will change.

I'm not suggesting that you go into denial or put on a brave face as a sacrifice, but consider the possibility that your words, thoughts, and perceptions are actually messages to your body.

If loved ones around you are dealing with health challenges, listen when they need to talk, but look at them and talk to them as if you are confident in their recovery. I don't mean to use words that deny their condition, but let the energy of your communication be one where you perceive them as they were, at their healthiest. Because inside, your Dad is still your Dad, for example. He isn't his illness. His spirit, his nature, is still the same holy, divine, beloved child of a Creator who only creates perfection.

Our earlier discussion of attachment to the physical body reflects this. It makes perfect sense that we identify with our bodies, and identify our loved ones with their bodies, but the spirit people encourage us to detach a bit if possible.

Staying Healthy

A woman in spirit told her daughter Helen who was taking on another certification in her nursing career, "If you become more involved in the responsibility for other peoples' well-being, take care not to become so involved in bringing other people to health that your own health is on the back burner. There comes a time when you have to put yourself first, and there is nothing wrong with that. You may feel a great responsibility *to* other people, but don't mistake that as responsibility *for* other people."

In a different reading for my client Christine, an aunt named Lucille came through from the spirit world. Christine was questioning her purpose in life, and whether she was making a difference. Her social work career was frustrating because the homeless population she served never seemed to diminish despite decades of effort, and she was starting to suffer from tremors and insomnia.

Her aunt Lucille's message began, "I see you as a lighthouse. You don't know how many people are seeing your light from a distance and being guided by it, but every once in a while you have to do maintenance on that lighthouse. You have to keep the lenses clean, you have to put in a new bulb, you have to make sure that all of the connections are still strong. If you don't, then the people who need your light aren't going to be able to see it. There's nothing self-serving about putting yourself at the top of the list, and maintaining your own lighthouse. That was a critical part of the job for old lighthouse keepers. Their job was to make sure the lighthouse functioned perfectly. Think about yourself that way. The lighthouse doesn't know how many people it's guiding, it's just there putting out light. That's all you have to know: your job is to put out that light and to make sure your light can shine as bright and as far as it can. Whether ships see it, use it, or don't isn't your concern. Your concern is to make sure that you shine."

***

My client Bill had lost his sister many years ago. He had originally come to me for hypnosis to help deal with the stress of caring for his mother, whose learned helplessness was becoming real emotional blackmail. When he discovered I was a medium, he made an appointment and expressed his hope that he would hear from his sister Penny. After he confirmed her identity through the various symbols, expressions, and connections she offered, Bill asked if Penny had an opinion about dealing with their mother.

"Penny shows me jumper cables," I said. "She says, 'When we hook up to the car that's actually running, all the juice goes to the car that isn't running, and it starts up. But it's important to unhook the cables from the strong car and let the weaker car charge itself, let the alternator kick in and start charging the battery, because if you keep them connected the stronger car is drained.'"

Bill said, "I was just showing my son how jumper cables work, so it makes sense that she would use this image. I was just explaining to him that you have to disconnect the cables because it's best for both cars that way."

"She continues, 'There's a connection that you can make, but it doesn't need to be sustained. Let our mother know the connection is here, but that she needs to run on her own a little. It's up to you now to build up and retain your own strength. Otherwise that one vehicle that's supplying everyone else with power is left with nothing. And the battery that's taking the charge can't even build up stored energy unless it starts moving.'"

Penny took the opportunity to advise her brother using an example that was present in his mind. Because he had just been explaining to his young son the importance of disconnecting the jumper cables – for the health and longevity of both batteries – this example was especially relevant. She recognized that the burden of their mother's care had been left with him, yet she encouraged him to disconnect and recharge from time to time for the benefit of both Bill and his mother.

***

In a final example of a self-care message, a woman in spirit came in giving me a sense of great irritation in my throat, which usually indicates a smoker. It was also difficult for me to breathe as I connected with her.

"This woman was intubated before passing. She couldn't breathe on her own. There was terrible discomfort in her throat."

"I think I know who you're talking about," said my client Arlene. "It could be one of two people."

"She gives me a feeling of medical intervention in her throat. She passed around retirement age, not elderly but past her working years, and being a little bit concerned about keeping up her appearance. She showed me coloring her hair well past the point when it was gray. She always had on some make-up."

"Okay, that's definitely my grandmother! It could have been my aunt, but as soon as you said 'keeping up her appearance' I knew that was her. She always said that exact line, 'keep up appearances.'"

"Your grandmother gives me the feeling that people took a lot from her. She gave and gave and gave. She shows me the symbol of being drained by a vampire. She shows this around you, too. Look at the outpouring of your energy. Look at one of your relationships and ask if it's totally draining you dry," I said to Arlene.

"Oh my God, that is so true," she replied.

"For you?" I asked.

"For both of us!"

"Grandmother's showing me this connection, this trait you two have in common. She wants me to caution you about overgiving, because you are doing this just as she did. She said there was no reward, just exhaustion. She used to enjoy giving but when the practice went from giving to being taken from, all the joy went away and she had a deep resentment."

"I can see where that's going," said Arlene.

"People came to expect she would always be available and would always do whatever was asked, and they kept asking for more. Even if she tried to say 'No,' she couldn't. This is the same in your relationship now," I said.

"It sure is," said Arlene.

"I just want to say one more thing from her because she's underscoring it. If you let yourself get into the habit of saying 'Yes,' it will be almost impossible to say 'No.' If you try to say 'No,' people will start saying you're selfish. That was her biggest sorrow before she died."

"What was?" she questioned.

"That people thought she was selfish in the end because she finally said 'No' to the big drain on her health and energy. Someone wanted her to continue to care for children, even after she was getting treatment for lung cancer!" This was remarkable news to me.

"That's right!" Arlene said.

"When she finally said 'No' because she didn't have the energy and needed to take care of herself, this person called her selfish. And she was sad about that at the end of her life, that after she died people would remember her as selfish." I said. "She doesn't care about that now in the spirit world, but she tells me it was heavy on her mind when she was sick."

"She still wanted people to think only good things about her," Arlene said.

"And the stress of that made her last days somewhat anxious," I replied. The grandmother stepped back but not before asserting once more that she carried none of that anxiety or stress into the spirit world, but instead had a healthier understanding of how including herself in those she cared for would have helped her in mind and body.

We put other people first more often than not, especially if we are caring for children or aging parents. Many of us put the boss first, either from a sense of insecurity about keeping a job, or because we feel subtly pressured into doing so. These clear messages from loved ones who have passed away touch on the unselfish nature of making our own health a priority, at least once in a while. We might feel despair that we can't help every sick child, homeless person, stray cat, or neglected corner of the environment, yet wiser minds tell us that we must tend to our own health with equal attention and to have faith that our efforts have a positive impact even if we can't see it.

Meditation for Physical Health (9:10)

As with any meditation (I'm using this term interchangeably with visualization and self-hypnosis), find the way the message works for you. If you are a visual person, picture the suggestions in your mind's eye. If you connect more to sound, imagine sound or vibration moving through you. If you're a feeling person, let yourself sense that you actually can feel what the meditation suggests. Feel free to adjust any of the wording to suit you. Meditation and self-hypnosis are not rocket science. You needn't perform perfectly every time, accept every suggestion one hundred percent, or try to force relaxation or images on your mind if you're resisting. This meditation takes approximately nine minutes, but can be shortened by skipping the relaxation countdown in the beginning. Relaxation isn't necessary for meditation or visualization, though you'll find it's a natural byproduct! Here are the keys to successful self-suggestion:

Every time you pay attention to an idea on purpose, with intention, it gets easier the next time. Repeat, repeat, repeat!

Use different images every time if you feel like it. There's no need to rigidly adhere to the same suggestions.

If something in this meditation doesn't quite resonate with you, tweak it. You must speak to your own subconscious mind in language or with examples you find believable or acceptable.

If you're creating your own script to follow for a specific medical condition, be sure to keep your suggestions in the present tense and defining the positive outcome. For example, say, "I'm getting healthier every day," rather than "I'm no longer sick."

If you'd like to, record yourself reading this script. Be sure to make any adjustments you think will be beneficial for your unique situation. Otherwise, have a general understanding of the path this script takes and recreate it in your mind. The words are not magic; if you don't recall it exactly during your meditation, that's okay. If you prefer to listen to a free recorded version of this script, go to: *http://liveandlearnguides.com/specialbookoffer/*

Some days you'll meditate easily and feel terrific. Other days you may only be able to settle in for a few minutes. That's okay. Repetition is more important than depth of trance.

Plan a time to do this. When we tell ourselves we're going to do something, we are more likely to follow through. Inform yourself that you will do this nightly as you're falling asleep, or sitting in the car for a few minutes before heading home from work.

If you're listening to the free recorded version you'll hear a tone before the relaxation countdown (*************) and again at the end. To skip the relaxation countdown, fast forward to the second tone and begin listening then.

Get comfortable, either sitting back or lying back. If you tend to fall asleep easily, try sitting up the first time. Close your eyes, and just breathe naturally and normally; you don't have to do anything special with your breath.

You are now using your mind on purpose, to create the kind of physical health you desire. You're now focusing your intentions and thoughts on adjusting the energies in your body so that you may recover and maintain your best health. You are getting closer, right now, to the healthiest you have ever been. It's simply a matter of your mind telling your body what to do.

(Skip the relaxation countdown between the asterisks if your time is limited or you tend to fall asleep easily)

****

As you count from 10 down to 1, all tension in your body will drain away. By the time you get to the number 1 you'll feel more relaxed than you've felt in a long time.

10: Imagine you're writing this number in black erasable marker on a whiteboard. Feel how easily the marker slides across the shiny surface; hear the little squeak of the pen. Maybe there's even a slight smell to this marker if it's brand new. Imagine you can see the number 10, just as you would write it. With your other hand now, imagine picking up the felt eraser and wiping the number 10 clean away. Notice that your shoulders and neck have become very relaxed.

9: Think about writing a 9 now. Choose a different color marker if you like, or stay with black. Look closely at the numeral 9 that you've written. It's very unique. No one else writes it as you do. With the eraser, wipe the 9 away. Your arms may be feeling heavy, or maybe light. In any case, they're getting more deeply relaxed now.

8: Make a number 8 on the white board now. Look closely at it. Does it stand up or tilt to the side. Are the curves at the top and bottom very round, or are they slim? Erase it now. I wonder if you'll notice that your back and hips are relaxing a little bit.

7: The magic number. Write a 7 on the white board. The simple act of writing this number seems to relax all the muscles in the front of your body. And your organs, as well. Just breathing naturally and normally, erase the 7.

6: Write the number 6 on the board and give it your full attention for a moment. Notice when you do that your legs feel very relaxed. Gently wipe the 6 away.

5: Imagine writing the numeral 5 on the whiteboard now, with it's angular top and round bottom. It's a funny looking symbol when you really think about it. Notice the number 5 makes your feet and toes relax. Erase the 5 you've written, and notice that the relaxation remains.

4: Think about writing a number 4 now. Picture it in your mind, see what color it is. Hear the crisp little 'click' as you imagine snapping the cap back on the marker. Erase the 4 you just wrote.

3: Writing the 3 on the board now, notice how calm and relaxed you feel. Notice that the relaxation you imagined has actually happened. You feel wonderful, at ease. Erase the 3 and notice the feeling of well-being remains.

2: Imagine writing a number 2 on the whiteboard. Look closely at it. See the unique way that you've written it. Wipe it away using the eraser in your other hand.

1: Make the simple, easy mark of a 1. Feeling completely relaxed, at ease, and ready to coach your body back to total health. Erase the numeral 1, imagine sitting back and relaxing even more.

****

In a moment you're going to imagine something—just play along, pretend if you have to. Using your imagination and concentrating are the two most important things you can do to get in tune with your body and suggest physical changes to it.

Imagine that there is a light in the middle of your chest, right where your heart is. Imagine that every time you inhale you're adding energy to that light—like old-fashioned bellows blowing gently on embers, oxygen feeds the fire making it glow brighter and grow stronger. Every time you breathe in, this light gets a little brighter and bigger. And every time your heart beats, it sends some of this light out into your body, along with healthy, oxygen-rich blood. It takes just three minutes for blood to be sent from your heart out to the very tips of your blood vessels and back again. Now your heart beats are sending light energy too, all the way down to the tips of your fingers and toes, and in three minutes, even less now, your whole entire body will be filled with this perfect glowing light. As you listen, this light continues to circulate through your body, bringing light, healing, and total relaxation.

If there is a specific part of your body that needs healing, bring that part to mind. Imagine the area around this part begins to pulse or vibrate very gently. With your attention there imagine a cool, comfortable beam of light coming down out of the Heavens directly into the place that needs healing. If your whole body needs healing, or a part you can't imagine specifically, picture that laser beam of light coming down right through the top of your head. Give that beam of light color. Some people see orange as a healing color. Others like green, or blue. Choose the color you feel like using right now; it may even change colors during this meditation. That's perfectly okay. Your mind knows exactly what to do, and your body knows exactly what it needs. You don't have to explain it or try to figure it out.

Allow this beam of light to target its healing right to the part of your body that needs it most. Picture it coming in, if you can. Think about all of your loved ones in the spirit world, and imagine them gathered around at the top of this beam, sending all of their energy down to you. Spirit people have extraordinary healing powers, and they can concentrate so much energy down to you. You can picture them all holding onto the top of the beam, or praying around it. You may even become aware of their subtle energy, too.

Let this light penetrate the part of your body that needs it most, for as long as is comfortable. You can imagine that body part begin to glow with the color of that laser beam if you like. This is very powerful healing energy, and many short sessions may be more comfortable than one long one.

As the laser beam cleans out this area of your body, think about all the cellular waste or debris, all the toxins, disease, or injury being zapped by this light. Just fizzling into nothingness.

Stay in the relaxed healing state for as long as you like. You may turn off the recording and drift into a comfortable sleep or come back to full awareness whenever you feel like it.

Or, if you're ready now, imagine the light beam softening and retracting back up to the Heavens. Let yourself accept that you have received a powerful healing. In a moment, you will reconnect to your active mind, feeling refreshed, relaxed, alert, and optimistic.

Take a deep breath, and exhale. Take one more, and locate your hands and feet, your arms and legs. Wiggle your toes or fingers if that's comfortable. One more deep breath, and eyes open, wide awake and alert. Every day in every way, you are getting healthier in body and mind.

Our Mental and Emotional Selves

Perceptions of Responsibility

Sometimes it's possible to confuse our degree of responsibility towards our fellow human beings. Care-taking is not equivalent to taking responsibility for someone. The spirit people seem to suggest that the point of care-taking and being of service is the act itself. Whether or not our intended audience benefits from the service we provide is not our responsibility to measure. As with Christine in the last chapter, she may not feel as though she is making a difference with the level of effort she is already expending, and in expending even more she exhausts herself and puts her own health at risk. She'd made the decision to spend more of her resources because she perceived her efforts were not enough. Yet the spirit people tell us that we shouldn't judge our efforts by whether or not people heal at a rate we determine to be the correct one.

In my work as a hypnotist, I have witnessed different examples of this confusion of effort. In some cases a level of co-dependence is involved. This occurs when a client may think that the most important thing she can do is to help her spouse quit drinking, and if he'd only quit for good they could finally begin to be happy. She overcares for behaviors that are not her responsibility. She attaches a great deal of weight to the desired outcome of her efforts. Her spouse won't fall or stand on his own efforts and she may be distracted from doing some deeper searching as to why she feels her life's work is to fix other people.

If we love the exercise of caring for its own sake, if we love to serve for its own reward, we almost always have a healthy detachment from how our clients or loved ones respond to our efforts.

Early in my practice as a hypnotist I thought that I'd failed if one of my clients didn't lose weight or quit smoking. In some cases, I was so invested in helping or "saving" someone that I'd take on the responsibility of doing his work for him. I had one client named Angela who wasn't getting any traction on her goal to get her own business off the ground. She felt some inner blocks. We worked on self-confidence, visualization, goal-setting, even past life regression. I would prepare for days in advance of our sessions, researching alternative ways to help Angela get started and gather the momentum to continue. And each time she came in she'd flop down in my chair and sigh, "It's not working." One of my mentors finally stepped in after the umpteenth time I'd asked him for guidance. He said, "That client is doing less work on her own goals than you are."

He was right! I was bending over backwards to help Angela, but I wasn't truly helping her at all. I was working harder on her advancement than she was, and I was losing sleep over it. When she came in for her next session, I asked how she had been applying some of the work we'd done. Was she listening to the recordings we made? Doing her self-hypnosis homework? Angela began protesting that she was too busy, her house was too noisy to concentrate, and for a number of reasons entirely beyond her control, no, she wasn't doing her homework. I let her know that, after that session, I wouldn't be treating her unless she was prepared to do at least as much work as I was towards achieving her goals. It came as no surprise to me that Angela never again called for another session.

Now when I see hypnosis clients I tell them before we even begin that I cannot quit smoking for them, or lose weight for them, and I won't promise any success unless they commit to the minimum level of involvement in their own treatment. More than one client has said to me then, "Will you guarantee that I'll quit smoking?" To which I reply, "I guarantee you'll quit smoking if you guarantee you'll do everything I tell you to do!" That is an effective way to weed out the motivated clients from the not-so-serious kind.

I offer this because I understand how easy it can be, especially for those in the care-taking or spiritual professions, to want to save the world and to tie up our idea of success with the results our clients experience. The wiser spirit people remind us that our job is not to measure the value of our service by the results of our clients.

***

Bonnie came for a reading on a weekend when I was visiting in another state. Several of her loved ones came through, whom she verified readily by the evidence they presented to me. I hadn't realized what an anxious state Bonnie had been in at the beginning of our reading; I'd assumed it was the general excitement and nervousness first-time medium visits can evoke. But as we came to the end of our time together, I noticed that Bonnie still seemed slightly on edge. At the time I was connecting Bonnie once again with her sister in spirit, who had been popping in and out of our reading from the start. I silently asked the spirit sister to pass on information that would ease Bonnie's tension.

"She shows me a light," I said, "and tells me that the light surrounds you. Everybody has this light. Sometimes we have to choose to look past a person's actions in order to see it." I wasn't sure where Bonnie's sister in spirit was going with this, but I noticed that Bonnie perked up quite a bit in response to this comment.

"How do I see the light?" she asked.

"What is broken about your daughter? Broken in her mind, I mean? Your sister shows me this."

"Yes, very," Bonnie answered.

"I have the feeling that your daughter's light is coming out in a different way. You have to perceive differently," I continued. "I'm not putting the burden on you, but I'm saying you won't see the light in her the same way you see it in another person. There's a beautiful soul in there, but what you're looking for in others you're not going to find in her. Not the same expression of it.

"I also see a lot of anger somewhere, in one person in particular in your family."

"Yes! My daughter. Hatred and anger," said Bonnie. "It's become clear that she is mentally ill."

"This feels like the broken part," I replied. "With a person who isn't broken we can draw love out in a relationship, but I don't feel that this is possible here. Your sister shows me, 'It doesn't mean there isn't love or she doesn't deserve love.' The efforts that would work with a person who isn't broken, aren't working here. Any more effort in this direction becomes excess."

"Efforts at love or efforts at trying to fix her?" Bonnie asked.

"Efforts at drawing a certain love from her," I continued, as her sister in spirit continued to put the message in my mind. She showed me an example spirit people have used before with me. "Consider an animal that isn't comfortable around humans. If it's a mammal I have something in common, and, with time, I can create an affectionate bond. I can receive love – or what I understand as love – from another mammal. However, if I'm interacting with an iguana, it has a brain that is different, and no matter how much I stroke it and feed it and pet it, it's not ever going to reciprocate. It doesn't have that type of a brain. I'm not comparing your daughter to a reptile, but the way we connect to most people may not be possible with your daughter. And that's not a failure on anyone's part, it's just the way it is. Your sister says, 'An iguana isn't a lesser example of God's creatures because it doesn't express itself the way a dog does, but it's unique and that's all there is to it. It doesn't make the person who raised the iguana a failure, because it isn't affectionate.'"

"I understand," said Bonnie. I turned off the recording at that time so we could talk about what this meant. I assured Bonnie that we don't have to follow the advice of spirit people. In many ways, their wisdom is out of reach of our abilities, and we shouldn't feel guilty if we're not always able to forgive, let go, or love differently. What her sister in spirit hoped to convey seemed to be that Bonnie manage her expectations regarding her daughter's emotional capabilities. Bonnie concurred that she had been feeling like a complete failure because of her inability to connect with her daughter the way she did with other family members. She felt a great peace after hearing from her sister in spirit. Knowing she could continue to love without expecting certain results lifted a great weight from her mind. She had perceived for so long that because she couldn't feel her daughter's love, she had failed in drawing love from her. Bonnie had taken responsibility for something beyond her control, and had been beating herself up about her "failure" for a long time.

The Power of the Intentional Mind

In the last section, we touched on co-dependence and how we sometimes unwittingly surrender our decision-making power. Marianne Williamson in *A Return to Love: Reflections on the Principles of "A Course in Miracles,"* writes "Our deepest fear is not that we are inadequate. Our deepest fear is that we are powerful beyond measure." Knowing how to use the mind to tap into that power means recognizing that we alone can set ourselves on the path of creation and achievement. Spirit people have plenty to say about the way we use our minds, too, and how much power we have over the course of our lives when we use our thinking minds constructively

In a private reading for Patty, her godfather Marcus came in with jokes and laughter, presenting himself the way he had much of his physical life. He also made a connection to Patty's mother who was recovering from hip replacement surgery. At the time of our reading Patty had just begun the first steps of starting a business after years of procrastination. She was finally beginning to gather momentum and confidence in her idea, but now felt anxious about getting off track. Patty knew that having to help her mother get to and from rehabilitation therapy, shop, cook for her, and process her insurance paperwork was going to be full-time work for the foreseeable future, and she was dispirited that her business idea would grind to a halt after she'd finally begun.

Her godfather had good news for her, though. He said, "What you're setting in motion will carry on. When you set something in motion, expect beneficial, far-reaching consequences. It's going forward on its own momentum." He encouraged Patty to keep the business alive in her mind and her intentions, even if she couldn't make any further tangible progress right away. It would keep her excited about returning to it, and the energetic form of the business idea wouldn't deflate in the meantime.

***

My client Chrissie received a similar message from her roommate Jen, who had passed away while both were still in college. After identifying her friend, Chrissie reminisced about the youthful nature of their friendship and the playful attitude they both had had towards the future. What's amazing about the following exchange is the wisdom of Jen's spirit. She was a young woman when she passed, not quite twenty years old, yet her message is one we might hear from an older mentor or someone with many more years of life experience.

"Don't screw it up," I found myself saying before I'd had a chance to filter my words.

"What?" Chrissie asked.

"Jen says not to screw it up, because this is going to be important for the next part of your life. Do you know what she's talking about?" I asked Chrissie.

"Maybe," she answered.

"She says, 'Just do it. Sit down and do it. Take care of business.' She's talking about you making a decision, getting off your rear and getting started. She says you're daydreaming a lot. She's talking about getting started on your future, about going back to school."

"That's what I thought," Chrissie sighed. "I keep thinking I'll go back and finish school, but friends tell me one thing, my stepdad tells me another, I have to save money..." She laughed ruefully.

"Jen says, 'Use your mind to decide what you want for yourself and then apply your mind to make sure it comes to you. Don't be lazy. Wish for things, but then apply yourself to getting them, too. Otherwise, time is going to go by and you'll still be wishing, "One day maybe this," "One day maybe that." Just take care of business. Decide what you need to get to the next step. Use your mind productively. Daydream productively, and get your work done.'"

Did Jen have this kind of wisdom deep within her as a teenager? Or did higher awareness come only after concluding her young life? Whatever the answer is, I personally feel encouraged that somewhere deep within us each of our spirits has this type of knowledge. Maybe we can learn to hear our own wiser mind instruct our intentional mind to create the motivation which we all need to accomplish our goals. If we all have this power within, as the author Marianne Williamson suggests, using the mind to tap into it means more creative control over the outcome.

***

Danicka's brother offered a similar message during a different reading. She was able to identify him right away when he came in announcing his passing from a brain aneurysm. In order to bring my attention to his name, he showed me a picture of a male baby.

"He's pointing to a little infant boy who was born since his passing. I think this is still a baby. This boy is here, he's not in the spirit world," I said to Danicka.

"I don't know any babies who passed away," she replied.

"No, he's definitely still here. When a spirit points to another name or another person, he means to refer to someone who is still here in the physical world. He makes a special connection to this baby. He tells me he and the baby have the same name. He's not showing me his name, just that he and the baby have the same name. He also shows me William Tell, but he highlights the 'Tell' part of it. Does this make sense to you?" I asked her.

"I named my son after him. He was born after my brother died. Is that what he means?"

"Your baby son was named after your brother?" I reiterated.

"Yes," she said.

"Does the 'Tell' part of William Tell make sense to you then? It doesn't make any sense to me, but he keeps underlining it."

"My son's name is Tellon," Danicka replied.

"Both your son and brother are named Tellon?" I asked. "Because I don't hear names in my mind's ear, the spirit people usually show me a saint or someone with a similar name to get me to say it. I don't know anyone named Tellon, so he got as close as he could with William Tell."

"We called him Tel for short," she said. Once we clearly established her brother's name, identity, and relationship to Danicka, he shared this message with her:

"He says, 'You don't realize the power of your mind to define your life experience.'"

"I'm feeling pretty bummed about things," Danicka replied. "My husband and I aren't going to stay married. I was going to go to cosmetology school but then I got pregnant so I had to put it off. Then we thought he'd help with the baby so I could go part time, but now he won't and I'm unable do it myself. None of my plans are working out and I feel like I'll never get going. I love my son, but I feel cheated. What about my dreams?"

"Drag it out of your mind and into reality. It's up to you to make it real. That's not coming from me, that's coming from your brother. He gets it where he is now. He understood a little of that when he was alive, but he understands it completely now," I said.

"He always did whatever he wanted," she told me. "He would go after anything he wanted, and get it. My mother used to say that everything he touched turned to gold."

"I think he knows what he's talking about then. He's showing me the time is going to pass anyway. He says you might as well apply yourself. Five years is going to pass anyway, so you might as well apply yourself so that you can say, 'Look, it took five years by I can finally work in this business now,' rather than still saying five years from now, 'I should really get this thing going.' Time is going to pass anyway. You're going to move along in your life anyway. You can make those dreams a reality. Be optimistic, don't be cynical. Keep the dream alive, but also recognize that dreams can be broken down into steps that you can take to make them come into the real world."

Tellon had an understanding of the power of dreams and intentions, but also the mental effort needed to bring them from the mind into reality. He even used the word "drag" to underscore that some force for mental discipline is required. He reminded his sister to dream big and stay optimistic, even though it can be challenging in the face of disappointments or delayed plans. It takes effort to stay engaged in our own futures, to avoid becoming cynical, and to keep our dreams alive. It takes effort to take action on those dreams, too.

***

Melanie's grandfather in spirit gave us more specific suggestions for grabbing hold of our own power. When she came for a reading with me, she was having trouble letting go of a long-held grudge with a family member. After being sure his identity was confirmed, her grandfather said, "Stop looking at the past. Stop trying to figure out where things didn't go right in the past. Take it from this moment forward. Set up a discipline now. A mental discipline becomes second nature, it will carry you through. Do this now, while you're young. You're investing in yourself, and you can draw on it when you're older. Start now."

As a former marine, this gentleman had learned a lot about discipline. He returned to this subject throughout our reading, applying it to every subject we covered. From his perspective, the more disciplined a person was, the less mental energy would be wasted.

***

My client Colleen came for a reading and was greeted right away by her aunt Ann. This spirit lady came through first and dominated throughout the session. Whenever I began to feel the approach of another spirit person, Ann shoved her way to the front of my awareness again. I soon understood that Ann wanted to act as a conduit for another female in spirit.

"Ann tells me she has to translate," I told Colleen. "I have the presence of another woman here who is trying to come in, but I can't connect with her directly. Ann says that's why she's here, to make the connection between us."

"Okay," answered Colleen. She hadn't had a reading before and I could tell she was deciding whether I was a kook or not.

"I can't communicate with her directly," I said again. "Ann is bringing in a second woman who died of a stroke recently, within the last few weeks."

Colleen acknowledged her mother, who was Ann's sister, had died a month ago from a stroke.

"This makes sense why Ann is here now," I told Colleen. "Some spirit people have told me that it's hard for them to connect directly if they've passed recently. I want to make sure that you are certain that this is your mother here with us." I asked Ann to ask the mother for an additional bit of evidence I could share with Colleen.

"She told me to mention a connection to Florida," I said, which Colleen validated without giving me further details.

"Now she shows me a flat bottom boat, the kind with the fan that is driven in the Everglades of Florida. She tells me, 'A boat that just skims across the water's surface is less stable.' She's speaking metaphorically to you and she wants you to commit yourself more, or to dive in a little deeper. Not to skim across the surface, because things are going to be less stable. She means a romantic relationship. She's saying, 'Don't skim across the surface because you'll end up feeling less stable.' It might feel safer if you don't get too deep or too intimate. but that's a false perception. Commit. If you're going to do something, jump in with both feet."

I continued on in this vein, as Colleen's mother kept underscoring the necessity of total mental commitment. I asked Colleen, "It seems to me she hopes you'll stop waffling and make a decision. You won't be able to fully indulge in all the power the decision has to offer if you can't commit to it. It appears you're always waiting for a better offer. You're hesitant about committing."

Clearly I was on to something, as Colleen had difficulty even committing an opinion to our dialogue. "Well, maybe," she whispered.

"Your aunt shows me your mother pointing to a man with an "ST" name like Steven or Stan. Do you know this name?"

"My boyfriend's name is Steven."

"I wonder what is the hesitation? I'm being shown that you can't make up your mind about Steven," I said.

"We talked about getting married, and I love him and everything, but my without my mom here to ask I just don't know. She always helped me in my big decisions," Colleen replied.

"Well, she's helping you now as an answer to that question in particular, but I see she also wants you to take more power in general."

Her mother then showed me swimming with dolphins. When I brought up this image to Colleen, she admitted that it had been a dream of hers since she was a little girl. "She's concerned that you've let go of a dream because everyone says, 'No, you can't do it.' Maybe not recapturing that desire to swim with dolphins, but the reaching-for-the-stars feeling. Letting yourself imagine any possible thing you would want to do for yourself without immediately saying, 'Oh, that'll never happen,' or, 'I don't have the money for that.' Be hopeful and positive. Don't lose that, because that was so admired about you when you were a child."

In her two symbolic examples, Colleen's mother was hoping to give her daughter courage to make her dreams a reality, and that commitment was her responsibility. She reminded us that if we just stay on the surface, we miss the benefits of total commitment, such as more stability and a deeper overall experience.

***

In a different setting, a devout spirit woman came in for the host of one of my message circles. Gina acknowledged her as an old family friend.

"I get the name Mary or Marie. Do you have someone with this name in the spirit world?" I asked. I had been shown the Blessed Virgin Mary at first to highlight this spirit's religious devotion, and the spirit had repeated it to show me her name.

"That's her name, Marie," replied Gina.

"She shows me a magic trick. The one when the magician makes something disappear under a handkerchief." I said. "She shows me this, but I don't think she's talking literally about magic. This is where I think she's going. Is there a conflict between what we're doing now [the message circle] and a [religious] belief?" I asked. I had a feeling I wasn't exactly on the right track, but as is common when translating non-verbal messages into words, some verbal massaging is necessary.

"No," said Gina, "I believe in this and I'm okay with it."

"She shows me magic but then she negates it. Marie says what's going on is not magic. It's real. I'm not sure why she's telling me this."

Gina, who has hosted messages circles before, remained quiet. She knew that as I spoke aloud the spirit would help me refine the message for her.

"Now I see an object which I feel has a symbolic meaning but I'm going to ask you if it has a literal reference first. Did you just open a fortune cookie?"

"Not recently," she answered.

"Okay, then I'm going to take it symbolically. She shows me a fortune. Are you expecting to have a sum of money come in?" I was going to get this message out if it took all night.

"No," said Gina. "But wait, I'm reading a book called *The Magic*, and it's about the law of attraction!"

"Okay!" I said, energy *zinging* up and down my spine as both the spirit and I celebrated the connection. "Thank you! Now we're getting somewhere. Marie is saying it's not magic, in reference to that book. She says, 'It's real.' By all means go on with that. Are you working it for prosperity?"

"Oh, yeah!" Gina replied.

"Go on with it," I said. "You got it right from Marie that it works."

Right in the middle of our message circle a spirit person took the opportunity to support her Gina's use of her intentional mind. By referring to something immediately relevant to her, her spirit friend showed us all that the powerful force of the mind can and should be harnessed for the betterment of our lives.

***

Another spirit person came through with a similar message at a different circle. Reyna's grandmother had been a bitter and sarcastic woman when alive, and Reyna was able to identify her right away when she offered as evidence a litany of familiar criticisms. Of course, the grandmother wasn't still criticizing family members, but only repeating some of the things she was known for saying before she passed. Once identified, she acknowledged that her cynicism and irascible nature made her difficult to tolerate, and she now showered blessings and love on Reyna. In defining her new understanding of how she was responsible for perpetuating her miseries while alive, the grandmother talked about how focusing on what made her unhappy extended and deepened her unhappiness.

"You got that right," said Reyna, who didn't even want to hear from her grandmother. Reyna had spent a lot of time in her grandmother's care as a child, and in her own words spent twice as many years in therapy to offset it.

"All she ever did was complain," Reyna said. "About my grandfather, my father, me, life, everything. God, she was miserable, and miserable to be around."

"She says if it weren't for bad luck, she'd have no luck at all," I said.

Reyna laughed and said, "She used to sing that song all the time."

"But now she sees life differently," I said. "She acknowledges that she went about it the wrong way. I mean she went about life the wrong way. She knows she brought all that unhappiness on herself because that's all she focused on."

"No kidding," said Reyna. It was clear the memory of her grandmother's personality left a sharp edge that hadn't softened in the years since her passing.

"She sees that you have a goal in your life and she doesn't want you to do what she did. She didn't have any power," I said. "Are you a photographer?" I asked.

"Workin' on it," answered Reyna.

"Your grandmother wants to give you some good advice, and she wants you to take it from someone who knows now what she didn't know then," I said. "She says being focused and designing your life is like turning the viewfinder on an image, getting it in focus and then keeping that picture in mind. And that is how we bring what's far away, closer to us."

***

Next is a final, unusual example of how spirit people advise us on the best use of the intentional mind. My new client Jason had come in desiring a psychic reading only. He was more interested in what was next for him in life and on a spiritual path. He described himself as a seeker, and told me he'd been exploring alternative thought for quite some time. During our reading I became aware of a woman in spirit, and asked Jason if I might bring her through for him.

"Do you know someone who had cancer twice?" I asked. "The first time overcame it, and the second time succumbed? I have this sharp pain in my lung or chest."

"Yes," he answered. "My wife had breast cancer."

"I feel this in my right breast," I said. "I want to make sure this is her. Was her cancer in the right breast?"

"Yes," he answered.

"Okay, I want to bring this person in," I said. "She shows me using her mind to imagine PacMan eating up the cancer cells, and that's how she beat it the first time. There's a message in this, to remember that your body only does what your mind tells it to, and you can create change in your physical body by using your mind as well."

"Okay," Jason replied.

"Here's what I see. I'm being shown that in this year, this next season of your life, you'll use your thinking mind and your subconscious mind in the right combination. Over the course of this year, you're going to find the sweet spot for what you think about, what you put mental energy into, and what just happens." I paused for a moment to make sure I was translating the spirit woman's message correctly.

"You're using both parts of your mind already, of course," I said. "I mean you won't feel as though you have to use one to connect to the other, or abandon one to achieve the other. You're going to use your mental force to create the things you can create. At the same time you'll see that your deeper, inner self doesn't need change or betterment. Instead of bringing about betterment, you let go of an idea about betterment. Does that make sense?"

"You mean integration?" he asked me.

"Exactly," I said. "You have this great mind and you can use it to create change. She shows me, 'This is where I'm going to use my mind and I'm not going to overthink the other stuff that is already naturally a part of who I am.' You don't have to work on perfection, holiness, and intuitiveness, because they already exist, but you can use your mind to work on other things. The effort goes in the right place, and nothing is spilled over.

"Your wife shows me this picture of your spirit being a cup that's already full, and the conscious mind pouring more water into it, saying, 'Let me make this better.' It's a waste because your spirit doesn't need betterment, it only needs recognition of its wholeness and perfection. Put the water over here where you can water habits or physical health. Put your mental effort into an idea you can actually add to. It's an 'Aha!' moment. Integration is a good word for that."

Jason's wife continued on for a little while to encourage his seeking, and remind him that he needn't seek spiritual perfection using the conscious mind. Instead, he could use his conscious mind in a way that would be productive for change where change was necessary or possible.

In all of these examples our spirit loved ones encourage us to be present with good cheer and to call ourselves to fresh efforts. They know that if we don't create change in our worlds others will do it for us, and we won't take full advantage of the great creative power we all have within. Using mental discipline, the Law of Attraction, and the simple act of focusing on what we want by keeping it in the forefront of the mind, we can do, have, and be all we could wish for.

Making Wishes

Reyna's mother came through after her grandmother finished her message. She was as encouraging as the grandmother in spirit had been. Both spirit women noted in Reyna a fatalistic attitude and offered her advice to turn it around, highlighting the value of intentional thinking and dreaming big. Much of their encouragement was around her work as a photographer. Once Reyna identified her mother, I began her message.

"She shows me Aladdin's lamp and says, 'Don't forget that you have wishes left,'" I said to Reyna. "She's reminding you that you can ask and wish for things. She shows me rubbing the lamp with your mind, attention, and focus. Don't give way to cynicism, stay wishful."

"My mother was the queen of wishful thinking," Reyna replied sardonically. "I love how my grandmother and mother are so cheery and upbeat, when they're the reason I'm cynical to begin with."

"Well, maybe they know better now. Spirit people frequently shine a light on how they had not been in life as a way of apologizing or saying, 'Don't be the way I was.' They can see now that their actions or attitudes caused much grief, and they don't want to see someone they love make the same mistakes they did.

"Your mother wants to say that the key thing about genies granting our wishes is that we define them. We have to articulate them. She indicates magic in declaring out loud. Don't forget that you have the ability to make your wishes come true. However, you have to speak them to give them energy."

"I don't believe in the whole affirmation thing," said Reyna.

"That's not quite what she means," I said, admitting perhaps I hadn't translated correctly. "Your mother reminds me that a problem defined is half-solved. She hopes you can have a big dream, especially about your creative work, and define some wishes you have about it, because once you start making wishes doors can open and what you are actively wishing for has a way to come to you."

I continued delivering messages for other guests in the circle, but before closing I was drawn to Reyna once more.

"Your mother has more to say," I told Reyna. "She seems intent on getting this message to you, so I'm going to address it one more time."

"Okay," she said.

"You got a message, maybe all girls got this message, about a fairy tale image of life. Then suddenly your mother told you, 'Grow up, stop fantasizing. Life isn't a fairy tale, there's no automatic happy ending.' She admits that after years of telling you that life was a happy story, she started ridiculing you for believing it. She didn't give you a new belief, she just told you you were stupid to believe in fairy tales. She's acknowledging a mixed message about this! She says, 'We told you to believe it, then suddenly we told you it wasn't true, but we never told you what to believe in instead.'"

"Right on," said Reyna.

"Your mother tells me she was wrong," I said. "She's saying, they can happen, the fairy tale can come true, but we have to actually play a part in it. The pages aren't going to turn for us, though."

"I don't even know what that means," Reyna said.

"She means first to acknowledge that you were in an impossible position. It wasn't your fault. She created a whole optimistic belief system for you, then destroyed it in one fell swoop; and, worse, she didn't help you replace it or build a new one. That's what she is acknowledging. If you can recapture that original belief system that magic does happen and fairy tales can come true and wishes are indeed worth indulging in, you will find the energy to pursue all of your dreams. And your dreams can also pursue you when you hold them in your mind with hopefulness and expectation."

I was quite moved by this mother's frank admission of failing her daughter when she was alive in the physical world. Reyna had such a hard shell around her, and it was easy to see why. She was raised by two bitter and disappointed women who seemed to revel in building up and then crushing her youthful expectations that life would be a fun adventure with many happy fairy tale endings. I left that circle hoping that Reyna and all of us who had the privilege to listen in on that message could recapture that youthful optimism. If Reyna could try picturing herself in her own fairy tale, as the Queen of All Photography, her mind might be more open to the magic of unexpected opportunities, creative ideas, new solutions to old problems, and most importantly, she would delight in all her successes and meet all of her challenges fearlessly.

***

I often wonder if the spirit people send their physical loved ones to me in groups, because for several weeks after Reyna's message the subject of wishes was a recurring theme. Not long after I met Reyna and her family in spirit I had a private reading in my home. Dean hadn't been for a reading in so long I didn't recognize him when he came to the door. He'd lost a lot weight, grown a shaggy beard, and looked rather haggard.

"I'm hoping to hear from someone in particular," said Dean after I'd brought in spirit people he immediately recognized. I closed my eyes and called out to the general spirit world for the one Dean hoped to hear from. I then saw the image of Eeyore from Winnie-The-Pooh. *Give me something else,* I demanded of the spirit.

"There's a man here but I can't yet tell what he wants me to say," I lied. *Come on, not Eeyore. What else?*

Eeyore, Eeyore, and more Eeyore. *Okay, I give,* I said in my mind. *Say "Uncle,"* I got from the spirit man. *Oh, I get it now,* I smiled to myself.

"The man here says he is your uncle." Dean's face immediately lit up.

"That's who I wanted to hear from!" he exclaimed.

"Well, he's here and he shows me Eeyore from Winnie-The-Pooh. I have no idea why, but that's what he shows me."

"He could imitate Eeyore's voice perfectly, and he used to make us kids laugh all the time," said Dean. "He would always tell us not to be downers, that the world has enough Eeyores. He always said if you can make people laugh you can change the world."

"He is also making a message out of it though," I said, explaining that spirit people do that quite frequently. They'll show some identifying characteristic, and then segue beautifully into a message based around that characteristic. Dean's uncle in spirit did this very skillfully.

"He wants you to consider that Eeyore had lost sight of all the happy things he could do in the Hundred Acre Wood. His friends were off eating honey and bouncing around, making all their wishes come true. This is an actual place you know," I said.

"What is?" Dean asked.

"The Hundred Acre Wood," I said. "It's a real place in England, which A.A. Milne made the setting for the Winnie-The-Pooh stories. Your uncle wants to remind you to buck up," I said.

"Oh my God, he used to say, 'Buck up, kid,' all the time!" said Dean.

"He shows me that you have this whole world, which is real but also make-believe, too. I hope I'm getting this feeling out the best way. If you are more like the other characters, like Owl or Tigger or the others, you'll find adventure even in the real world. Buck up and try to be more optimistic. I think that's what he saying," I said.

"I guess I need that right now," Dean sighed. "I've been feeling pretty pessimistic. Sometimes I just feel that life isn't working out, so I stopped caring about trying to make it work out."

"He wants me to answer that by saying, 'Don't forget that you have wishes and that you can ask for things. You don't have to be so black and white.'"

"I'm definitely black and white. My wife tells me that all the time. She says if I don't get one hundred percent, I act as though I got nothing," Dean admitted.

"Bring some wishful thinking back in. Your wishes are going to be granted, so if you wish for things just know that. Wishing puts you in the mind of creating and hopefulness. Don't forget to have wishes."

***

In one particularly poignant reading, my client's mother came through. She'd committed suicide by hanging herself, and the entire family was experiencing intense pain. No one had ever suspected that she would take her own life. The fact of her suicide and the impression my client had of her mother created such a cognitive dissonance that my client was having an extremely difficult time. She validated her mother almost instantly, and begged her mother in spirit to explain why she'd killed herself.

"She shows me a genie in a bottle," I said, understanding by this symbol that I would soon be talking about wishes. "I see the genie giving three wishes. We're reminded that we have three wishes. It can also mean for a spirit person, 'I had three chances.' Did she have three episodes of a problem? She wished and prayed to get better and she did, and the second time she wished and prayed and also got better, but the third time it didn't happen, she didn't get better."

"Yes," answered my client.

"She expands on this a little. She shows it as three chances, or for her, three wishes. Where she is in the spirit world now she can see that when she was alive she didn't think she had more wishes or more chances, and this is part of what played into her decision. She thought, 'It's all downhill from here. It's hopeless from here.' She also wasn't thinking clearly; she shows me a fog or a mist. 'I can't see through the mist. I couldn't see. There were more opportunities for me, there were more chances, but I couldn't see it.'"

"She was sick, and she was getting treatment for the third time," my client said. "We never expected this. Did she think she was going to die?"

"She shows me she wasn't thinking clearly," I answered, "so, yes, she felt that this decision was the best one for her. I feel this heavy mist around her."

"She was taking a lot of medication and she didn't like it," my client offered.

"There were more opportunities for her, but she couldn't see them, maybe because of this mist," I continued. "She recognizes that now where she is. Her message is not to forget that are always more more chances."

Knowing we have wishes or chances available to us in the future gives us a reason to go on. Sometimes it's a matter of life and death, as in the example above. Wishing is a powerful tool we've been given to create or escape to a hopeful, optimistic, and self-empowering place. The spirit people urge us to never underestimate the power of wishing.

I've seen the value of creative thinking through daydreaming and wishes in many spirit communication examples. Wishing contributes to our joy and happy expectation, and with an outlook such as this we are more likely to use our intentional minds to take action towards our goals. This happy outlook results in a feeling of control and empowerment, allowing us to tolerate mistakes we or others make. Young children love fairy tales because they engage the creative mind and outline the importance of being our own heroes. They make heroic action believable. Armed with that kind of confidence and desire we truly can do anything.

The Power of Choosing

In a private reading last Spring, my client Jenny's sister came through from the spirit world describing herself as being one who got up on the wrong side of the bed and who never got back into bed to get up on the right side. By the time she passed away, her pessimistic mindset was such that she could not get outside of it to view her circumstances differently.

"Your sister tells me that the end of her life was a great relief," I said. "She says, 'I'm glad that's over!' Next time she's going to come in and get up on the right side of the bed."

"I hope so, for her sake," Jenny answered. "None of us could understand why she was so pessimistic."

"She had no other frame of reference, and is asking for acceptance of that part of her. She wasn't designed to be a down-in-the-dumps person. It became hard to step outside and look at life differently." Her sister showed me herself seeing life through a periscope that could only see the negative side. "She couldn't step outside of her own state of mind. She is free and happy now."

"My sister had a real 'victim' mentality," said Jenny.

"Now she's underscoring the importance of choosing how to see things. She says, 'If you get up on the wrong side of the bed, even for a half hour, see if you can take that half hour back and restart.' For a mentally healthy person, it can be done. It's crucial to do that. If you've been focusing more on the fault side or what's going wrong – well, it's necessary to acknowledge those things, but after that withdraw all of your attention from the negative."

"She couldn't do that when she was alive."

"From where she is now she can see that. She says it had become her habit to draw the short straw or always get the raw deal."

"That's for sure!" Jenny answered.

"Now she sees that sometimes we have to make a decision – and it can be challenging – to see what is positive. When we do, that kind of seeing becomes a habit and expands."

This young woman in spirit had spent much of her adult life focusing on how life was disappointing her, and it wasn't until she got into the spirit world that she saw how she could have changed that. To clarify, Jenny's sister wasn't clinically depressed when alive, only one who always saw the glass as half-empty. It is not easy or always possible to change how you look at things when struggling with a chemical imbalance. In her case though, she could see that she had gotten into the habit of negativity, and had abdicated responsibility for her decisions.

A few moments later in the same reading a male came through and identified himself as Jenny's uncle. He showed himself with prostate cancer.

"He says he was unable to speak in the end," I said to Jenny.

"Yes, that's right," she said.

"He shows me his throat, shows me looking down his throat. This is strange. I think he means to say he couldn't swallow."

"He wanted to be able to swallow pills to take his own life when his cancer advanced," said Jenny, "but by the time he made his decision it was too late. He couldn't swallow, so he had to live out his life in hospice."

"He comes in immediately after your sister because he has a follow-up, and it's interesting that you gave me his history. Where your sister said we have choices in the way we look at life, he's saying, living or not living our life is a choice also.

"Often we don't realize we have a choice, because we're acting out of habit. Together they're suggesting that we look at everything that is going on as a result of decisions we have made, or decisions we're making in the moment, or setting ourselves up for decisions we'll have to make in the future. Both are showing us that everything you have from the mental state to whether or not you're alive comes down to decisions that you make. If you understand that, it's extremely empowering to set up things the way you want them to be. Even if it's simply perceiving how you're going to feel about a distressing situation, your choice is your own. That is the only authentic control we have, but it can extend to our entire lives."

"This is just what I needed to hear," said Jenny.

***

At another time, a spirit grandmother came through during a one-on-one reading with my client Agnes. She spoke eloquently about choosing to come into physical life:

"She says, 'I expected to experience spirituality physically, but I couldn't do it because that was perception and not knowledge. I perceived things through my body and didn't realize my body was simply a way to learn, and not my real experience.'" Not sure I'd said that correctly, I asked the spirit to give me another example.

"Your grandmother is encouraging a non-identification with the body or the physical experience – not the shape, but the physical experience – because that's where we perceive things," I said. "She wants me to say, 'Be careful not to misidentify with the body. The body does nothing on its own. It is only a tool for the mind to use. The mind is the creative part and the body does not stand separately apart from the mind.' The body only does what the mind tells it to do. Therefore, it's important to recognize that the body has to exist in order for the mind to exercise creativity. The spirit tells the mind what to do. The spirit is already created and already complete. The mind creates action using the body."

Agnes is a student of many spiritual philosophies, so even though the message I was sharing was rather cumbersome, she understood the gist of what her grandmother in spirit was telling her.

She continued on to teach both my client and me: "We are alive in two ways: physically and in the spirit. The spirit doesn't need to create because it's already created. So identifying with the spirit is better than identifying with the body or the mind."

"What am I supposed to do with this knowledge?" Agnes asked.

"She wants me to say, 'Your job is to recognize your spirit and recognize that it doesn't need correction or action. You already know your spirit, you've just forgotten it's wholeness and perfection. Let your prayer be to remember who you truly are, and to remember that your mind is just a tool. Your body and the physical world are places to use that tool. The mind is a bridge between who we perceive ourselves to be and what we can actually do in the world."

"I think I understand that," Agnes replied.

"The message is very complex, but the bottom-line feeling I'm getting from her is that we have to choose which aspect of ourselves to put our energy into. We must choose to focus on the spirit, remembering that it isn't broken and doesn't need fixing. If we perceive brokenness or incompleteness, we're incorrectly focusing on the mind, which is fabricating."

I see clients for both readings and hypnosis, and the majority of them struggle with low self-regard. This message from Agnes' grandmother is such good news! Who we truly are is already whole and complete. If we consciously choose to turn our thoughts to this awareness and don't focus on perceived lack, we will realize our beauty and power.

***

During a message circle a couple of years ago, I brought in the spirit of a young man who struggled mentally at the time of his passing. This was not a case of chemical imbalance or diagnosed mental illness. This spirit claimed he was locked in a cycle of bad decisions. My client, his brother, identified him immediately.

"He's acknowledging that he had made some poor decisions, one of which caused his death. He also tells me that his family and friends were baffled by his actions and choices," I said.

"That's putting it mildly," my client replied, shaking his head. "We joked about putting 'What the Hell Were You Thinking?' on his headstone, because we were always asking that."

"He's trying to describe his mental challenges," I said.

"Good luck!" my client joked.

"This is not mental imbalance though, he says. He says, 'Mental challenges.'"

"Okay."

"He's trying to show his mental challenges, using a beam on a fulcrum, and that his balance was off because the fulcrum was off. This is a symbol for his mind. He says, 'It was so much work to be in balance.' Especially once he was off balance he made choices that overcompensated, and put him totally off balance in another way," I said. "You guys couldn't understand because your fulcrums are in the right place to keep all your thoughts and emotions in homeostasis."

"He did some whacky stuff," my client responded.

"Your brother says that because he felt naturally out of balance, it was a huge effort to feel and act normal. He realized he was making bad decisions but it was hard to act from a place of sensibleness."

"We tried to help him."

"He agrees with you. He says, 'I didn't start it, but I didn't stop it.'"

This is a representative sample of the many messages I've translated on the topic of making decisions. Spirit people touch on their choices or their loved ones' choices in probably ninety percent of my readings and circles. The spirit people frequently acknowledge their use or misuse of choice, and craft their own experience into helpful information for those of us still here. Knowing that much of our lives are shaped by the act of choosing, we are empowered to create comfortable inner and outer environments – and the spirit people make every effort to remind us of this.

Taking Risks and Overcoming Fear

The spirit people reflect not only on making decisions, but on making mistakes. In this section, we'll hear what the spirits have to offer on overcoming fear, taking risks, and having the confidence to move in the direction of our goals.

Norma's father came through in a message circle composed of a group of her friends and co-workers. She acknowledged his identifying details: that he was a paratrooper in the service, that he felt he was at his best when he was in the military, and that, as a father, he felt himself in unfamiliar territory.

"He gives me a booze-y feeling, too," I said. "I feel a bit muddled, as if I'm drunk."

"That's him, he was an alcoholic," Norma replied.

"He wouldn't have said that about himself, but we would say that about him today. He shows that he let his health and responsibilities slide.

"He tells me, 'Don't be afraid the way I was, and if you have to parachute into unknown territory, just do it.'" I waited for him to be more specific, but he stopped right there. This type of statement is rather generic, the sort that comes from unskilled or even fake mediums. I like to give detailed messages that speak to the unique lives of each client, so I waited for a finer point to come through. It seemed this father wasn't giving me anything else, however.

"I know exactly what he's talking about," said Norma. I waited for her to fill in some of the blanks, too. Apparently, she wasn't going to give me much more than her father had.

"Don't be in denial, don't let your fear define or rule you. He means to say this about insecurities as well as fears. He wants to say, 'Don't do what I did. I didn't know what I was doing, and I didn't know how to cope and the ways that I knew how to cope destroyed my body.' He is encouraging you to be fearless, and not to worry," I said.

Norma identified with his message immediately, though I didn't get the details until some time later. In an email a few weeks after the circle, Norma told me she was on the threshold of coming out as a lesbian to her family and friends, and had been anxious that they wouldn't accept her after her news. She admitted her drinking was increasing, as a way to deny or avoid living freely as her authentic self. Her father's message gave her courage and confidence, and ultimately helped me to understand why neither one of them was more specific in the giving or receiving of a message I thought was too generic.

Using his own life as an example of what not to do, Norma's father was able to identify himself, acknowledge his shortcomings as a father, and offer helpful support to his daughter. Hearing words of encouragement she never heard when he was alive gave Norma a sense of connection and guidance when she needed it most. The spirit people don't usually show regret or apologize because in spirit they see things differently, but they do acknowledge where they fell short when alive. They more frequently craft a message from the "Don't Do What I Did" column than from the "Do As I Did" column. Perhaps in the spirit world it is possible to see that no risk is too great if it means living authentically and fully.

***

My client Audrey's grandfather came through in a family reading. He showed himself as a farmer, which she validated. He then commented on her new efforts towards natural, healthy organic foods by saying, "This is how we did it back then, now you young kids are finally getting back to what we already know." He showed us his warm sense of humor, and then grew somewhat serious. He prepared to get his message across, and it had both a literal and symbolic connection.

"Were you in gymnastics when you were little?" I asked.

"Yes!" she said.

"He's showing me gymnastics first as a way to make a connection to you, but also because he wants to teach us. He says, 'When you had to learn the balance beam it was on the floor, right?'"

"That's right," Audrey answered.

"He continues, 'You learned to do your moves with the balance beam on the floor where it wouldn't hurt if you fell off. Then when it's raised up higher to the standard height, your mind is already conditioned that it doesn't hurt to fall. You're conditioned for confidence.'"

"Yes, that's exactly how we got to be more confident on the balance beam," she replied.

"He's saying, 'The risk that you're taking, or the leaps that you're taking – remember it's a matter of your mental perspective, too. Be confident about your decision.'"

Not sure if I got the point across, I said, "I'm totally bumbling this message."

"And I'm totally getting it!" Audrey said, smiling. At a crossroads in her small business, Audrey was hoping to expand but felt the risks might be too great. As she said to me after the reading, "I was worrying out loud to my husband and said exactly the words, 'The higher I go the farther I could fall.'"

Audrey's grandfather knew that the courage to take a leap can be either diminished or strengthened by the right mental perspective. He wasn't advising fearlessness per se, but rather that she consider the source of her fears when making decisions. If fear is simply a matter of adjusting her mental perspective, it is within her power to change it, just as she had when she was a girl learning gymnastics.

Making Decisions and Making Mistakes

My new client Sue clearly had something on her mind when she came in for a reading one day last winter.

"What's going on?" I asked her.

She laughed and said, "You tell me."

"Oh, so it's going to be one of *those* readings!" I replied, smiling. As soon as we began an elderly spirit man approached.

"He's quite intellectual. He shows me a bright mind, well into old age. He passes in his late eighties or early nineties, and his mind is sharp the entire time. He's wearing a plaid flannel shirt, and he has a pocket protector with pens in it. I see dollar signs, a symbol of a banker or one who worked with money. He also shows me Massachusetts."

Sue acknowledged a great uncle on her mother's side of the family.

"He's expressing confidence in your ability to be resolute and to make decisions," I said. "Does this make sense?"

"It sure does," she said.

"He's confident you can move forward in ways that are pleasing to you and satisfying. He says, 'Life isn't a chess game.' You don't always have to figure out a person's next move before making a move yourself. You're creating the future by confidently stepping forward and making a decision. Every time you make a decision, an entirely new gameboard appears.

"He says the great strategists who play chess are thinking, 'If I move this piece, then my opponent could do this, then if he did that, then I could do this.' They play out all the way to checkmate in this fashion. But in life this strategy keeps us in one place because we're just speculating about the way life can go. There are many more factors, not simply one other player. Instead, make a move, make a decision. You'll have a whole new set of opportunities then."

"He actually loved to play chess," Sue replied.

"It would make sense that he would use this example," I told her. "Spirit people often use their physical experience to create a message."

Sue then told me she had "paralysis by analysis." Unable to decide about the next steps in several areas of her life, she found herself going around in circles rather than moving forward, exactly as her great uncle defined. With his reminder that the chessboard resets itself every time a decision is made, Sue felt more confident about choosing without second-guessing.

When we manage to avoid second-guessing ourselves and choose with confidence, even bad decisions can be a positive experience. Spirit people tell us that poor choices may *send* us into the spirit world, but they don't *follow* us into the spirit world.

***

During a one-on-one reading with Lena, a spirit came through showing himself as a healthy man in the prime of life.

"He's lean and athletic. He's never been sick a day in his life," I said. "Next he shows me an episode of what he thought was heartburn or indigestion, which he expected to diminish. Then he has a sudden, shocking, fatal heart attack. More shocking because of his presumed excellent health."

"That's my dad," said Lena, able to identify him right away because the cause of his passing seemed so antithetical to his lifestyle. After a few moments of personal messages for Lena, her son, and her mother, the father in spirit brought in another male whom Lena could not immediately identify. This spirit had taken his own life with a gun.

"I have the feeling of someone who died as a result of a gunshot. It doesn't feel like a crime. I see cleaning a gun. He tried to make it appear to be an accident but there was some intent behind it."

"I don't know who that is," she said.

"Someone who knows you and whom you would know, comes in and gives me this picture of himself," I persisted.

"Not at all," Lena said.

"I'm not sure where he comes from. I won't spend any more time on him," I said. It's possible that I misconstrue a spirit or definition, so I attempted to put him aside in order to continue with other spirit people. This man in spirit wasn't going to be brushed off that easily however.

"He was accused of something he didn't do, a person who said, 'He harassed me.' It was connected to work. He became depressed and was either laid off or involved in a scandal. He became more and more withdrawn, and then had a subconscious 'accident' in which his life was lost, involving a gun."

Lena stared silently at me. Once again I tried to dismiss this spirit, yet again he persisted.

"It's your father who brings this person through," I said. "Maybe he worked with your father, or your father knew him through work. Float it by other family members, to see if your father ever mentioned someone like this," I suggested.

"Okay," she said, "but I can't think of anyone."

"It's important that the information comes through. Your father is presenting this other man as an example. He says, 'We are not punished for even the most dire mistakes we make.' Our spirits are not punished. It's we who punish ourselves, and there is no judgment or reprisal in the spirit world. Maybe you heard, 'If you kill yourself you're in limbo for eternity.' Your dad's clear message is that everybody knows the love of the spirit world or the love of God. Everybody, to the same degree, experiences that peace and serenity.

"He's also including self-judgment. If you judge yourself harshly, he's saying, 'Let it go. There is no judgment.' The harshest judgments are self-imposed, and even if self-judgment is so extreme a man takes his own life, God would never reject him. God would never judge us, so we must refrain from judging ourselves.

"Maybe your father had a similar feeling himself, or maybe you do about yourself, but he's saying very, very clearly, to release the self-judgment, release the harsh criticism. If you've made mistakes, forget it, move on, don't worry about it. That stuff doesn't go with you. It only goes with you in life, and that's only if you carry it emotionally. If you can let it go, then you're going to have a much better experience, and more of a Heaven-on-Earth experience, because in Heaven that doesn't happen."

"I am hard on myself," Lena responded. "I look around and think I would be a lot farther along if I'd made different decisions when I was younger."

"Well, maybe your father's bringing in this spirit as an extreme example of what 'hard on yourself' can turn into. He says, 'God's not hard on you.' If God wouldn't punish you, don't punish yourself. God knows better than you!" We closed the reading shortly after this strong message, and several days afterwards Lena called to tell me that after talking with her mother she was able to identify the spirit man who had died of an accidental gunshot wound.

My client's father saw in his daughter that she was holding herself to an impossible standard, and brought in another spirit who had done so to the extreme. He was sure to convey that if a suicide were accepted in Heaven, Lena would be, too, and she should ease up on herself. In a way, he was saying that no self-imposed judgment is so important that we should punish ourselves if we seem to fall short.

***

The last example in this section comes from a message circle that I held for a small family group in their home, and relates to the nuts and bolts of moving confidently towards goals. One of the guests was able to identify her mother-in-law in spirit immediately.

"She shows me a pool table," I said, "and I'm waiting to discover whether this is an image for me to take literally or if it is symbolic. I sense she is going to tell a story with this."

"Well, none of us here play pool," the guest replied. "Maybe it isn't her?"

"Let's wait and see. I'm going to get this message out and maybe it will make more sense.

"This lady means to make a suggestion," I continued. "She tells me, 'If you want to get a ball into one pocket it's not aligned with, you have to not shoot for the hole.' She says that you have to expect that the ball is going to glance off the bumper and travel in another direction. She's talking about aiming for a goal."

"That could be anything," my guest answered.

"Yes, it could," I agreed. "But she is standing right in front of you and she is referring to a goal you have stopped aiming for, because you can see that your first efforts won't land you there."

I opened my eyes to look at my guest, who was starting to look a little bit uncomfortable.

"She shows me this way of setting up a shot and says, 'Sometimes you can get more accomplished if you work like that, rather than aiming directly. Put your effort into an action that will cause another action.'"

"Okay, I get it," my guest said. "You don't have to say any more."

"Oh, but she wants me to!" I laughed. "She's encouraging. If a goal seems to be an impossible shot, instead of aiming straight for it, aim for a step that can lead to that goal. I think she's talking specifically about you going to school to finish first one diploma and then another one. She shows me two diplomas.

"Maybe her message means breaking larger goals down into shorter steps. Just focus your energy on the first step. She doesn't think you're seeing the bigger picture, which she does where she is."

"Well, okay, since she's not going to shut up about it!" said my guest to the other family members. "I've been thinking about going to school for nursing."

"That's great!" was her sister's reply. She went on to encourage her plans, knowing she already had an Associates Degree.

"The thing is... I haven't actually finished my first degree. I never got it. I left before I totally finished, so I have to go finish that first and then start looking at nursing school." She explained that she was embarrassed about having been untruthful about the first degree, and was thinking about dropping her bigger goal altogether. Hearing from her mother-in-law in spirit encouraged my guest to believe she could achieve her larger goal, even if it didn't seem so at the outset.

When it comes to ownership of our lives, our loved ones in the spirit world constantly encourage us to be bold, to be ourselves, to worry less about what other people are going to do, or how we need to strategize to make sure we avoid mistakes. If we listen to them, we know the biggest regrets come from fear of making mistakes or fear of judgment. If we learn how to operate from the place where our true desires emanate, and to carry out those desires with a resolute heart, we can enjoy all the benefits of Heaven on earth.

Grief, Guilt, and Letting Go

Grief is one of the hardest emotions to navigate. Everyone experiences it differently. Because of some cultural discomfort with the subject, grief can be a heavy weight that many people bury deep inside their hearts. We know the spirit people speak of reunion and the immortality of the spirit, and try their hardest to give us hope during the times we feel separated from our loved ones by death

During a private reading with a middle-aged woman, her mother in spirit came to join us. My client identified her through the various bits of evidence she offered. Once I and the spirit mother were both sure the connection was accurate, her message came through.

"This lady shows me a sculpture of a Victorian angel on a grave, weeping. She is showing me a symbol of grief," I said. "She's representing suffering with this symbol."

My client confirmed that her mother had had a very difficult life.

"The feeling is profoundly heavy," I continued. "The statue represents sorrow or grief. No matter how beautifully carved statue is, it's a heavy, granite, weighted-down burden. That's what grief is."

My client was clearly quite upset at this point, and I suspected that though the mother's symbol was about herself, the description contained a clear message for her daughter.

"She says, 'Try not to give sorrow weight. Instead, give sorrow to the angels, who are light. Light will carry our sorrows away, while giving them weight will tie us down.'

"Your mother shows me she had a hard life that was a great burden. But where she is now she says, 'If we could look at these burdens differently, and give them to angels or give them to God, they will take flight and leave us, and they'll be where they belong. With real angels, and not with our representations of angels.'"

"She was really into angels," said my client. "I am, too. We used to give them to each other."

"This is why your mother is using this particular example. It makes sense that she would use a symbol that's meaningful to you both to illustrate her message," I replied. "She's making a contrast between how we perceive grief and how it could be instead." I started to laugh at this notion, because the spirit people deposit such extraordinary insights into my field of understanding, which are difficult to convey accurately.

"Spirits put these amazing ideas in my head and I have such a hard time articulating them," I told my guest. "In short, she says that even though we all feel sorrow, 'Don't memorialize grief, but let the angels lift the burden and carry it away.' You have to give it to them, and not hang on to it as a memorial carved in stone of someone you loved."

***

The subject of grief came up in another reading shortly after that, which is of no surprise to me anymore. The spirit people seem to know which subjects the clients struggle with, and maybe they give their physical loved ones a nudge to get in touch with a medium. It's quite interesting when a spirit comes through opining on a particular topic, and for the next several weeks other spirits connected to other clients expand on that topic. For example, if I have a spirit who committed suicide and comes through to bring understanding to my client, a huge percentage of subsequent readings also result in suicides coming through with similar messages. So when the topic of grief came up almost immediately in a subsequent reading, I was ready to give the message and learn more about how to handle this difficult emotion.

Crystal and I were on the phone for our reading, when she brought up her perceived inability to stop grieving. It was a challenge to even define the source of her grief, as she was feeling stuck and unable to process her sadness and move on.

She said, "I'm grieving, and can't get over it."

After identifying many of her spirit people, the whole group of them shared this message.

"They're telling me that grief naturally pools as rainwater does," I said. "If we have good drainage it moves through us; it fills up and drains away. But if we don't have energy moving through us it can pool up and get swampy and heavy. All we see is this pool of grief and we begin to stare into it as Narcissus did. It can become a little bit self-indulgent. We're not honoring the people we're missing, the times of our lives that have changed, or the future that's waiting for us."

None of the spirit people suggested Crystal bury or deny her grief, but rather that she find a way to move through it. Knowing she would be honoring them more by expressing her grief and letting it pass, rather than keeping it alive as a memorial, Crystal felt refreshed and optimistic about letting her usually cheerful nature surface once more.

Guilt feelings can be as difficult to process as grief. Spirit people have often chided my clients about indulging in guilt. Because it can feel oddly comforting to revisit episodes that created guilt feelings, it can be particularly hard to let that heavy emotion go. Many of my clients have expressed their fear that releasing feelings of guilt will be dishonoring a lost loved one. We see similar expressions around grief; we've probably all met someone who believes that forgetting their grief is equivalent to forgetting their loved one. Yet the spirit people tell us again and again that we aren't honoring them by being stuck in either grief or guilt. They are most assuredly not upset if we laugh or smile again, or fall in love again; no spirit child has ever been upset that his parents in the physical world had another baby to replace him.

***

My client Sharlene was part of a message circle composed of her work colleagues. When her grandfather came through, she was able to identify him right away by the pictures he gave me of his life in Haiti and his emigration to the United States.

"He shows me that he either caused someone's death by the water," I said, "or he couldn't save someone near the water."

"I know that story," Sharlene replied. "It was a family secret for awhile but eventually it came out and I got all the details after he died."

"He carried a tremendous amount of guilt over this failure to prevent a death," I said. "That's what he wants to talk about, the guilt."

"That I don't know about," she said.

"He says, 'We burden ourselves, and when we get into the spirit world there is no burden,'" I continued. "He truly understands now that his guilt has no weight or value out there. He says, 'Don't judge yourself so harshly.'"

"That makes sense," Sharlene answered.

"You are the only one carrying that burden, and why drag it all through life only to get to Heaven and understand, 'I didn't have to do that,'" I said. Using himself as an example, he gave Sharlene permission to let go of her own self-persecution.

***

Three young women came for a message circle earlier this year. It's hard to believe college and high school students have an interest in spirit communication, but this particular group was engaging, articulate, and immensely interested in the process of communication with the deceased. Grandmothers, grandfathers, aunts, and uncles came through, and we were having a wonderful time at this family reunion. Just as I was about to end our session, I felt the presence of a young man who was not a family member.

"He shows me he's at the outer edge of the circle," I said to Sonia. "He's not family, but probably an acquaintance or a friend of a friend." Spirit people often place themselves at varying distances from the client, who is at the center of a circle I see in my mind's eye. Family will be close by the client, while friends and more distant family members position themselves slightly farther away.

"He had a head injury – this feels like recklessness," I said. "He is your peer, around your age, he gives me the feeling of a blow to the

head. I see a motorcycle... no, it's an ATV. He shows me being in a
coma, in suspended animation. He shows life support and a decision
to stop medical care. I'm talking about pulling the plug."

"I'm not sure who that is," said Sonia, looking over at her two
friends. All three looked puzzled. "I think we would remember
someone like that."

I asked the spirit man for more information. "He points to the
name 'Martin,'" I said.

"Oh, okay!" Sonia cried. "I know who that is now!"

"Who is this man to you?" I asked, curious about the connection
to the name Martin.

"My friend Martin had a good friend who just died," she
answered. "It was as you said. He was riding around during the last
snowstorm before the streets were plowed. Nobody knows how he
flipped. They just found him on the ground."

"This young man shows me he was brain dead, in a coma on life
support," I reiterated.

"Yes," Sonia answered. "And his family finally let him go about a
month ago."

"Do you still talk to Martin?" I asked Sonia, knowing that this
young man had a message for him.

"Sure," she replied.

"I see that Martin is carrying a heavy guilt about this," I said.
"Were they together? He shows me someone with him. He shows me
Martin thinks he could have prevented this or responded differently."

"Yeah, I think so," answered Sonia.

"Listen, if you think it's appropriate, please let Martin listen to this
part of the recording," I said to Sonia, referring to the MP3 audio file
I create for every reading and circle. "His friend wants Martin to let
go of the guilt. This man is taking full responsibility for his actions.
He's fully accountable. He doesn't want anyone to think that he
should have done something to stop it."

"Okay, I'll tell him," she said.

"Really, please do," I urged her. "He's insisting. Martin is not only
grieving but is carrying guilt, and his friend in the spirit world needs
him to know that he sees and feels it, and it isn't serving either one

of them. 'Martin is still alive!' he says. 'Don't give up your life just because it appears I gave up mine.'"

Revisiting guilt can be like probing a sore tooth with your tongue. It's painful, yet we can't resist doing it. This is why the spirits encourage us not to indulge in guilt. They are not lost to death, we still have living to do, and when we get out to the spirit world we'll understand that carrying feelings of guilt was a complete waste of our energy. It doesn't come with us into the afterlife, and we don't earn points by keeping it alive. The spirit people tell us if we've truly made an error, accept it, learn from it, and move on. Continually beating ourselves up for past behavior isn't going to make us better people, it's only going to make the rest of our lives boring and miserable.

***

When we move difficult emotions through the expression process, we benefit. There's also wisdom in not stirring the pot, as the spirit people illustrated during a reading with my client Remy. I sensed resistance and wariness from Remy, so I asked her spirit people to be simple and clear with us when they came in. Though extremely skeptical at first, Remy identified her mother quite easily when she came through. We got right down to the message once her identity was firmly established through the multiple bits of evidence offered.

"She shows me a depth finder," I said to Remy. "Do you know what this is?"

"Oh yes!" she replied. "My parents had a boat at their place on the shore, and they used their depth finder when they went fishing. I don't know why she'd show me that; it wasn't significant or anything."

"Maybe she means to use it as a message," I said. "Spirit people will often show something connected to them, and then expand it into a vehicle for their message. I can see on the depth finder screen things that swim at a very deep level. Your mother says it's not always healthy to pull deep things up to a shallower surface level."

"What does that mean?" asked Remy.

"She says, 'Sometimes we can let sleeping dogs lie.' Not everything has to be brought up and examined. Everything you do doesn't have to be overanalyzed. Some things happen on the surface and they can stay there; some things happen very deep and they can stay there, too."

When I opened my eyes Remy was looking at me, but the skeptical shell had fallen away and she was a little teary.

I continued, "She suggests leaving old hurts or wounds buried, if you have them. Nobody's going to benefit from dragging them up. She's talking about relating to somebody. It isn't always the answer, to ask, 'Why did you do this?' or, 'Why did that happen?'"

"I've been doing that with my father," said Remy. "When he left my mother – this was years and years ago – it was hard for all of us. We were all pretty angry about it. Now that she's gone I've been angry at him again for leaving her."

"If she is saying, 'Leave it alone,' you might consider letting bygones be bygones. It seems pretty clear that she's not angry, and I feel she's saying that dragging up an old betrayal from so long ago is only going to keep hurt alive. If you processed your anger and grief about it back then, no need to dredge it up now."

Maybe we don't always know when to let go of grief, guilt, or pain, or when old hurts heal. We do know from the spirit people themselves that we might try to move through those difficult emotions rather than carry them with us. In the spirit world all negative interactions and emotions are forgiven and forgotten, so if we can let them go while we're here in the physical world, perhaps our day-to-day lives will be lighter and more joyous.

Expectations of the Mind and Spirit

We can use our minds to do some extraordinary things. The power of positive thinking has healed the sick, elevated people out of poverty, and driven amazing social, physical, and spiritual change. The spirit people applaud our efforts to create joy and achieve goals, but also caution that the same powerful mind can do the opposite if we're not vigilant.

One of my regular clients brought along a friend named Cara whom I'd never read before. After explaining the process of mediumship and how I worked in particular, I opened the door for the spirit people to enter.

The first to come in was a woman connected to Cara. I described an elderly lady who experienced declining health due to diabetes. After lapsing into a diabetic coma around the age of ninety-one, her granddaughter, my new guest Cara, allowed medical intervention to cease. Usually clients like this carry some degree of guilt about their actions, but not Cara. She was struggling with a different issue. As I began to translate her grandmother's message, it became clear that the spirit was using her own example to urge change for Cara.

"She had an expectation that wasn't realized," I said, after the grandmother had been clearly identified. "She shows me a pregnancy that didn't come to pass, but it's metaphorical, she's creating a symbol out of this image.

"She says that what she planned and fantasized about just evaporated. She shows me a deep disappointment." Cara continued to regard me without offering any feedback. I asked the grandmother why she was showing me this symbol.

"She says, 'I was anticipating a certain life, but that was my mistake. I was expecting *another* life that I thought I'd step into, instead of living my own.'"

"I don't get it," Cara said.

"Me, neither!" I replied. "Let me ask her to clarify." I asked the grandmother to spell out exactly what she wanted me to convey to Cara.

"She tells me someone who is carrying a child is expecting another life. That's the symbolic way she tells me, 'I should have spent my time creating my own life. It would never have been a disappointment or an unfulfilled expectation.'

"She talks about the mind's ability to create experiences, but also its laziness when it's only creating expectations. 'I should have created my own life and instead of trying to get by on expectations.' She says others' expectations are not within your control, but creating and choosing your thoughts is. If you try to coast along with unexamined expectations of your own, just by default, you may be disappointed. Instead, think with purpose. Take control," I finished, hoping I'd done justice to the piece of her knowledge the grandmother gave me to translate.

"Does that make sense to you?" I asked Cara.

"You have no idea," she replied. Cara confessed to being disappointed by yet another personal relationship that didn't mesh with her expectations. The two ladies laughed for a moment about co-dependent romances. I could see that her grandmother's message gave Cara hope and inspiration to set old expectations aside, and begin defining her life on her terms.

***

I had the privilege to deliver a similar message in a one-on-one reading one rainy Saturday morning. It was a day in late winter when the slush hadn't quite gone away, the sky had been overcast for days, and everyone was feeling grumpy. My client was able to identify her great aunt after the spirit offered several pieces of specific information.

"This is a bitter, disappointed lady," I said. "Makes sense she'd come in on a day like today."

"Exactly," Karen answered.

"She shows me she took neither credit nor blame. She was a victim of her circumstances or the times. There was always some reason outside of herself why her expectations were unfulfilled," I continued. "She has a learned helplessness or acquired victimhood."

"God, she was miserable to be around," Karen volunteered.

"She says, 'Despite my environment, I still had choices, but it was easier for me not to make them.' She's acknowledging this now from the spirit world."

"Does that do her any good now?" Karen laughed.

"Well, I think it's going to do us some good," I said, "because she's flipping her experience around into a message. She says, 'You're always going to be halfway there.'"

"That's going to do us some good?" Karen cried. "God, that sounds just like her to say something so discouraging."

"No, she's laughing, she means it differently," I replied. "What she means is don't be satisfied or settle. But also don't be discouraged because 'I'm not there yet.' If you think, 'I'm always halfway there,' you'll be motivated to continue. She says that to motivate you to keep going and to manage your expectations. She shows me sometimes you are driven by achievement, achievement, achievement, but still not feeling satisfied."

Karen didn't reply, but she was holding her face in her hands.

"She's encouraging awareness of your choices. She hopes you choose to see yourself halfway there, to keep yourself motivated to continue and also recognize how far you've come. Your success is on a continuum, and you don't see all the successes that brought you halfway to where you want to go. Instead, you are focusing on how much farther you have left, and feeling unfinished until you get there. But she says we never get 'there.' We're always halfway, because we keep reinventing things. You have an expectation that your success is a series of finished achievements, but your grandmother says you could take care to consider how much fun it is to be halfway there."

With a deep sigh, Karen looked up and agreed she needed to hear this message exactly as it came through. And so did I. As the translator from spirit-impression to verbal communication, I have the privilege of witnessing wisdom even while I'm the one conveying it. Sometimes I hijack a message and take a little for myself to reflect on later, and I hope the spirit people and my clients don't mind. When I hear advice from someone who has learned from experience, the message automatically carries more weight. We can all learn to enjoy the continuum of success, and because this message came from a woman who wasn't able to do so when she was alive, I feel a greater sense of purpose or urgency. There's no message more meaningful than one from someone – here or in spirit – who has learned from his mistakes.

***

A fine artist named Ariel comes for readings now and again, and on one particular occasion her dear friend Jan came through with a message about the mind.

"She gives me a feeling that you are one wavelength with the water or nature. You know this feeling, right?" I asked her.

Ariel nodded.

"'Therein lies the key,' she says. 'I don't know where I end and the environment begins.'" As neither of us was making much immediate sense of this example, I asked Jan in spirit to expand a bit.

"That feeling is an elementary step to a more permanent one. It will not ever be a lasting experience – that oneness – because we're here, in the physical. But you can achieve a semi-permanent or a voluntary jaunt to this feeling, and here in this feeling is where everybody who has ever advanced has downloaded things that already exist." It began to dawn on both of us that her friend was talking about an idea like the collective unconscious. According to one dictionary, the collective unconscious is "in Jungian psychology, a part of the unconscious mind, shared by a society, a people, or all humankind, that is the product of ancestral experience and contains such concepts as science, religion, and morality."

"She's talking about the feeling when you are outside alone in nature, everything inside is so still you feel you're one with the atmosphere. As though you have no physical boundaries. That feeling is an elementary step; right now it's a momentary feeling because we can't sustain it. We can never as living human beings enter this state in a permanent way because we have a physical body and an active mind," I said.

"I started meditating again in a more serious way, asking for more connection," Ariel replied. "I know the feeling she's talking about."

"The more often you can attain that feeling, the longer you'll be able to sustain it. In that feeling-place you are aware of your wholeness. That state of mind is true awareness that you are already perfect and fully realized," I continued.

"Your friend shows me people on the leading edge of technology, art, and music. They didn't invent or create themselves, they attained this feeling and accessed or downloaded those new ideas. Beethoven, Einstein, Marie Curie, she shows me scientists, musicians, artists, athletes.... A 'genius' is not intellectually so bright, but a genius can not-analyze. She can achieve a certain state of mind, get out of her own way, and then take what she downloads and put it out into the world. This step of not-analyzing has to be taken in order to do that download. You can develop yourself by recreating that feeling even in your imagination."

"In meditation?" Ariel asked.

"However you get there. It happens randomly. Sometimes you get there on purpose, but more often when you just stop and look around and realize everything matches. It's not the analysis of that. Right now you can achieve that for a moment purposely in meditation. She's not talking about going there or getting there, but about stopping everything. It's recognition. Silence isn't necessary. Everything is exactly how it's supposed to be right this minute," I said, amazed at this information that was coming out of my own mouth. In a way I was witnessing what Jan in spirit was saying, without truly understanding it or processing it rationally while I was speaking. Translating what Jan was saying so rapidly without processing it intellectually myself had me feeling as though I was trying to catch up, just as Ariel was.

"She wants to be more specific," I said. "We can't think ourselves into that. That's what she means about genius. The genius doesn't analyze herself into this creative state but leaves the thinking mind out of it during that process. In that oneness a transfer occurs. Then the mind comes back in to take that data and put it out into the world."

Both of us were feeling pretty frustrated with this high-level message, so I asked Jan in spirit to present her message more simply.

"I see a picture of a chimney flue," I said, in response to the new information Jan was giving me. "The mechanics of the flue are like the mind: whether it falls open, randomly opens, or we find a way to open it, data comes down. Then the flue closes and we have material to work with.

"All of the great advances, scientific, musical, artistic, are accomplished because someone has gotten into this state and was able to check in and access what has already been created. Everything has already been created. The alpha and omega, beginning and end. It's the I Am. And, endeavoring to get out of your own way so that this can come down is the practice. Set aside the expectations, analysis, and the seeking of balance so you can find perfection in spirit. We don't need to seek spiritual or artistic perfection because it's already there. We need to let it happen," I continued, as Jan continued to flood my mouth with words.

"Okay," replied Ariel.

"We need to be, not do. We reach this feeling when we sense we're one in the environment," I said, reflecting back on what Jan had first taught us. "We can expand or revisit that more often. Let that be the goal. Look for this experience. Not to create a great painting, get along with a particular person, or earn more money, but to make your experience, focus, or intention only to *be*. Then your perception shifts and it becomes unnecessary to seek what you thought you needed to find, such as balance or perfection."

"It's hard to digest," Ariel said.

"Because it's not an intellectual exercise, she tells me. She's talking about the appropriate time to not use your mind, in order to bring things into your mind."

Every time I read this section, I'm astounded at the wisdom of the spirit people. They try to guide us in so many ways, to help us fully realize our joy and purpose. In the following case, a spirit person puts some complex ideas about the mind and the spirit into a clear message.

***

Robert and I were having a wonderful time connecting with his people in spirit. His uncle came through, an engineer who was proud of his intellectual ability.

"He says he was a genius," I told Robert.

"Oh yes, that's him. He was extremely smart," Robert replied.

"He's talking about the power of the mind, and the appropriate investment in the training of the power of the mind, but the mind is not the most important thing. The spirit is the most important thing." I let this sit for a minute, absorbing the message myself and making sure the spirit uncle had no corrections to my translation.

"He says, 'The mind has creative ability and creative power, and we can do amazing things with the mind, but we have to realize that it's not the Almighty. The spirit is beyond creation, beyond analysis, so it's important to realize the mind comes along for the ride in the body,'" I said.

Both Robert and I asked for some clarification, and his uncle told us more.

"He tells me, 'The spirit is the alpha and omega, it is always there and always perfect, so our mind should serve our spirit, not serve itself. We should use our minds to remember that our spirit needs no correction. If we sense that correction is necessary, that is the mind referring to itself, or serving itself. The mind can help the body and create the lifestyle, but the mind should not simply serve itself. He encourages the development of the rational, conscious, analytical mind, but he says it's just a part of our whole experience here and it's best used to direct the body and actions, but not to interfere with the spirit. It's a misuse of the mind to find fault in the spirit."

"Will you ask him what he means by that?" asked Robert. "I don't get how the mind shouldn't serve itself."

"Let's see what he has to say," I replied as I tuned back in to his uncle in spirit. "I think he's showing me that when the mind serves itself, we think that intellectual advancement is the way to measure goodness or 'betterness.' We can use our minds to bring great things into our lives, but sometimes we do that because we think a vital part is missing or broken. This can lead to fear, feelings of inadequacy, all kinds of problems. Then the mind goes into a more intense version of striving towards 'betterness' by fixing what it determines to be wrong or broken. All the while the spirit, the real engine of life, runs along perfectly without any flaws. The spirit doesn't need fixing, because it's perfect. The mind when it serves itself instead of the spirit, focuses on the incomplete power of intellect. When the mind serves the spirit those corrections and drives all fall away. We know inner harmony, and then we can see and experience harmony everywhere."

"Okay, I think I get that," said Robert.

"The mind doesn't create harmony," I continued. "Your uncle shows me that, and says he knows that now where he is. He says the mind thinks it can create harmony when it's serving itself. When it serves the spirit, it is recognizing Divine harmony, and that's a lot less work."

Robert and I continued to discuss this message for a while after his reading was over. His uncle's message was so relevant, it may have instantly cleared away long-held self-worth issues in both of us!

Our loved ones in the afterlife are eager to instruct us on the best ways to use our bodies and minds. In the next section you'll read some astounding messages about our spiritual selves.

Meditation for A Healthy Mind (10:00)

As with the Meditation for Physical Health, find the way the message works for you. If you are a visual person, picture the suggestions in your mind's eye. If you connect more to sound, imagine sound or vibration moving through you. If you're a feeling person, let yourself sense that you actually can feel what the meditation suggests. Feel free to adjust any of the wording to suit you. Meditation and self-hypnosis are not rocket science. You needn't perform perfectly every time, accept every suggestion one hundred percent, or try to force relaxation or images on your mind if you're resisting. The following meditation takes ten minutes, but can be shortened by skipping the relaxation countdown in the beginning. Relaxation isn't necessary for meditation or visualization, though you'll find it's a natural byproduct! Here are the keys to successful self-suggestion:

Every time you pay attention to an idea on purpose, with intention, it gets easier the next time. Repeat, repeat, repeat!

Use different images every time if you feel more comfortable. There's no need to rigidly adhere to the same suggestions.

If a part this meditation doesn't quite resonate with you, tweak it. You must speak to your own subconscious mind in language or with examples you find believable or acceptable.

If you're creating your own script to follow for a specific condition, be sure to keep your suggestions in the present tense and define the positive outcome. For example, rather than saying "I'm not thinking about failure," say "I have confidence in the power of my mind to create change,"

If you'd like to, record yourself reading this script. Be sure to make any adjustments you think will be beneficial for your unique situation. Otherwise, have a general understanding of the path this script takes and recreate it in your mind. The words are not magic; if you don't recall it exactly during your meditation, that's okay. If you prefer to listen to a free recorded version of this script, go to: *http://liveandlearnguides.com/specialbookoffer/*

Some days you'll meditate easily and feel terrific. Other days you may only be able to settle in for a few minutes. Accept that. Repetition is more important than depth of trance.

Plan a time to meditate. When we tell ourselves we're going to do something, we are more likely to follow through. Inform yourself that you will do this nightly as you're falling asleep, or sitting in the car for a few minutes before heading home from work.

If you're listening to the free recorded version you'll hear a tone before the relaxation countdown (***************) and again at the end. To skip the relaxation countdown, fast forward to the second tone and begin listening then.

Get comfortable, either sitting back or lying back. If you tend to fall asleep easily, try sitting up the first time. Close your eyes, and just breathe naturally and normally; you don't have to do anything special with your breath.

You are now using your mind for a set purpose, to reinforce the right use of the mind. You're now using your mind to create responses and reactions that bring you closer to your goals. You are getting more traction on your dreams right now. You are releasing anxiety and stress. You are turning your attention to those things you can control, and comfortably and safely letting go of those things you cannot.

(Skip the section between the asterisks if your time is limited or you tend to fall asleep easily)

****

As you count from 10 down to 1, all tension in your body will drain away. By the time you get to the number 1 you'll be more relaxed than you've felt in a long time.

10: Imagine lying back in a comfortable inflatable boat close to shore. The weather is perfect. You are completely safe. The sun feels so pleasantly warm on your skin.

9: The boat begins to drift along, taking you on a nice, lazy journey. The rhythm of the water beneath the boat gently rocks you in a daydream state of mind. Birds are singing in the trees, white puffy clouds are floating by. You have all the time in the world.

8: As you let yourself be carried along, drifting and dreaming, you find your body naturally relaxing.

7: The sun feels so good, all the tension in your muscles just melts away. Your shoulders, back and arms feel so very relaxed.

6: Drifting and dreaming, your hips and legs relax. Imagine you can just let your head fall back against the warm, soft side of the inflatable boat. All the muscles in your neck, jaw, and throat relax. The sun on your face feels so wonderful.

5: Drifting along, feeling the gentle rhythm of the water beneath you. Hearing the birds somewhere in the trees, you relax even more.

4: Imagine the boat comes to an easy stop in the center of a clear, shallow pool. The sun is dappling the smooth rocks on the bottom of the pool. Sunlight dances and sparkles on the surface of the water. The movement of the sunlight's reflections is mesmerizing, and so very relaxing.

3: You are so comfortable in this warm, sunny place, with sunlight twinkling all around you. So very relaxed and peaceful. You notice that all the reflections of sunlight begin to run together, until it seems like you are right in the middle of a reflection, yourself.

2: Picture that light dancing all around you, forming a cloud of light all around you. This cloud of light is ready to reflect all you wish to project onto it, because it's a reflection of the inner You, the receptive mind.

1: Breathe naturally and normally. Feel your powerful mind prepare to project positive, efficient, and acceptable instructions onto your receptive inner mind.

****

*You're comfortable, at ease, and relaxed. You have total power over your mind and emotions. **You** make those unique and powerful decisions. Imagine a clear white screen in front of you, made up totally of reflected light. Anything is possible here – as long as you decide to put it there.*

Imagine now that you can project something very specific onto this screen. Whatever you place here must be adopted and performed by all the parts of your subconscious mind. Think of yourself as the captain high up on the bridge of a ship, while down below in the engine room the crew is busy performing their various tasks. Think about how, as captain, you have a clear destination in mind. You look at the charts, select your destination, and then determine the best way to navigate there. From where you are, you alone can see the horizon. You alone can see obstacles or objective hazards along the way. In order for you to reach your destination safely, it's imperative that the crew in the engine room follow your commands exactly. They cannot see what you can; they can only follow orders.

*Your subconscious mind is made up of many parts acting just like a ship's crew, all following instructions until they are told to do otherwise. The problem is, sometimes these instructions were given a long time ago and are no longer relevant. Or perhaps they were given when you were too young to challenge authority. But you're the captain now. What you say, goes. Without question. The subconscious parts of your mind **must do** what you instruct.*

Take a moment now to consider a part of yourself that you know to be an obstacle. Maybe you criticize yourself a lot. Maybe you sabotage your efforts to eat healthy foods and achieve a comfortable weight. Maybe you keep picking the wrong sort of person to fall in love with. We all have parts that are working under old instructions. People who are victims in life allow their crew steer the ship. You are a victor; you're assuming your rightful place at the helm now. No more sailing in circles, going back over the same old ground. Let's take time to inform the individual crew members what their instructions are.

*Imagine the first one stands before you now. Take a moment to understand what the behavior, activity, or reaction is that you wish to correct. You don't need to know **why** this part of you does that, or where it came from. Just look clearly at what it is. Now, very gently and in your mind's voice, change the job description of this part. For example, if you are nervous around authority figures because your self-esteem is shaky, call that part in front of you, and notice what happens when you feel that part taking over. Now, firmly tell this part of yourself, "The next time you have to deal with authority, take a deep breath, stand up straight, and square your shoulders. You feel confidence increasing. You easily remember and articulate all that you need to say. You remain calm, cool, and in control."*

*This is just an example. Speak to each part firmly, clearly, and repeat your instructions a couple of times. Make sure the instructions are issued in the present tense, and describe the positive way you will respond **now.***

****

Pause here to take as much time as you need. If you're listening to the pre-recorded version, you can pause that recording now for as long as you like.

****

When you've created instructions for your new responses, call one more part of your mind to your attention. This is the part that decides if you have control over something or not. The part that clearly and correctly understands whether or not you can change the outcome of a situation. This part can look any way you like.

Be very clear with your new instructions now. Imagine you can look this part of you squarely in the eye and say, "From now on, your job is to clearly inform me on the right action to take if I have control over a situation. If I don't have control over a situation, your job is to make that crystal clear to all the levels of my mind, and allow me to carry on comfortably."

Send this crew member back down below to get right to work carrying out the new rules. See yourself once again at the helm, looking towards the horizon, making your way towards your goals. Feel the happy confidence of one who is secure in the knowledge that you are clear in your mind, and focused in your efforts.

Take a long, deep breath in, and exhale. Wiggle your toes and fingers. Stretch your arms and legs. One more deep breath, eyes open, smiling, optimistic, confident in the power of your mind.

Our Spiritual Selves

Communicating

Any advice on relationships seems to boil down to one thing: communication. It's so important that, without it, we can't achieve the high standard of understanding and compassion that makes up the healthiest loving relationships. And communication is more than a two-way street. We have to know and love ourselves well enough before we can hope to share real intimacy with another. We have to communicate within our spiritual selves to articulate our dreams, to make peace with the past if necessary, and to develop our intuition as a useful tool. One of the greatest burdens my clients seem to carry is anxiety or sorrow resulting from unspoken forgiveness or apology. They are worried that because communication with a loved one in spirit had broken down somehow before death, the client remains unforgiven or the spirit remains unsettled.

During one message circle, my guest Sarah acknowledged the presence of her father. "I see he passed before his time," I said. "Spirit people use this phrase when people said this about them after they passed. Usually because they were 'too young.' He is showing me former military, specifically the navy. I also feel booze-y," I said, "and that means he was a drinker."

"That's my father," Sarah sighed.

"Now he's talking about himself and the family," I said slowly, as I waited for the feeling he was giving me to expand a bit. "But he's talking about sweeping things under the rug."

"I'm not sure what that means," she replied.

"He says, 'When you sweep something under the rug, the only thing that happens is the floor becomes more uneven.' He's asking you to deal with things that need to be dealt with, rather than putting them aside. Don't ignore them. The family needs to talk about a particular issue, and he says, 'All this does is make the surface treacherous to walk on, because now you have lumps in the rug that you could trip over.'"

"Now I know what he means," said Sarah. "My family never talks about anything."

"There's only benefit in getting everything out in the open," I continued. "He's saying if negative emotions come up when you talk, the feeling of those emotions, of fear, isn't life-threatening. As uncomfortable as that may sometimes be, it's much more comfortable and safe and secure, after the fact. He's urging communication about the difficult things, because it's just going to make the path you're walking that much smoother and easier. It's just going to make your house neater. Don't sweep things under the rug, don't ignore things, and you'll find that your way is easier. Once you get into the habit of speaking honestly or communicating clearly, then that becomes second nature and almost guarantees a smoother road."

Sarah recognized the relevance and timeliness of her father's message. Another family member was also drinking heavily, and rather than confront the person, most members of her family chose to look the other way. As Sarah said, "We deal with problems by ignoring them."

Her father in spirit learned from his own mistakes and tried in his message to prevent his living loved ones from repeating them. He acknowledged that the family's fear of his own temper had set the stage for denial, avoidance, and enabling, and he admitted that he made it difficult for his children to communicate honestly with him. Anyone who brought up his drinking inside or outside the home was severely punished. Now the remaining members of his family were stuck in a culture of ignoring issues that affected them all, and, as her father mentioned, making the road even bumpier. Sarah considered sharing the recording of our circle with her family, in hopes that it might launch a new strategy of communicating openly and fearlessly.

***

In a similar reading, my client Shelley's maternal grandfather came in.

"He is showing me lung cancer, twice," I said. Shelley acknowledged that he was treated twice for lung cancer.

"He shows me that he liked to drink beer," I said. "He's not a drunk, he just likes to have a beer." I paused as the next picture began to form in my mind's eye.

"He's showing me your toys coming to life," I said. "Does this make sense to you? Or did you just take out some of your old childhood toys?"

"No," Shelley answered, "but when I was a kid it was a huge fear of mine that my toys would come to life and act on their own. He knew that."

"I get two parts to this message," I replied. "First to connect to you through this personal knowledge he has about you. Second, he shows me an issue that you need to talk about. He shows me that saying, 'There's a big elephant in the room that nobody's talking about.' He's indicating something that wasn't talked about and gives me a feeling of it being in the family. I think he's talking about fear."

"Oh, well, we've been living with the elephant forever," Shelley said.

"He is cautioning you against that," I continued. "Maybe there was some fear or shame attached to it. He's saying when things come up for you it's more important to face them and talk about them. Otherwise, we forget how much of an impact that can have on our lives. If we don't integrate things that happened in the past, then we forget them and we run the risk of repeating them."

"I get it," said Shelley.

"He says, 'Don't let there be any elephants in your room.' Lay it all out on the table, because otherwise you carry fear all through your life. Once you're in the spirit world you know, 'Oh, that was no big deal, I didn't have to be afraid of that.' He's give me the feeling of being free," I said.

As we talked more about the subject of old fears, it became clear that this grandfather cautioned against getting comfortable with the elephant in the room because it took up space that could have been used for joy, creativity, and learning. Spirit people seem to share a common theme in all their messages, which is one of living authentically, and being ourselves without shame or fear, guilt or worry. With our human ability to communicate, spirit people show us the key to the fully-realized self is partly in being fearless about looking honestly at everything. Last week a father in spirit came through in a phone reading, showing me his hands over his eyes, similar to the see-no-evil monkey. To his son, my client, I said, "He's saying, 'Don't do this.' Don't put your head in the sand. He wants you to look closely, don't ignore a problem. Lay everything on the table and have a clear look at things. I see a stack of papers and he wants you to lay everything out at once and just look at it honestly."

His son knew what the father was referencing – his state of denial about financial obligations that weren't being met. My client's father urged his son to pull out all the relevant paperwork, overcome his anxieties and dive right in to discover the actual state of his financial affairs. Only then could he be open to communicating the need for help or more time from his creditors.

***

Regarding the how-to's of communication, one uncle in spirit provided a relevant message to his niece.

"He shows me bowling and wants to say, 'It's more about technique than brute strength.' He wishes you to consider finesse or technique, and not power."

"I haven't been able to persuade my sister regarding our mother's care," my client answered.

"What you're struggling with now, your uncle says, 'Less force, more technique.' We knock down more pins, or get more of what we want, by putting a slight spin on the ball, rather than just heaving it out there."

"I understand," she answered.

***

Lastly, advice on communicating came in for an international client of mine named Aline. During our phone reading the matriarch of her family came in with specific characteristics that Aline identified and validated immediately. Though uneducated, her great-grandmother in spirit had wisdom to share and got right to the point with Aline.

"She says sometimes we look at people not for who they currently are, but for who they've been to us in the past, and this generates expectations which aren't always realistic. Your great-grandmother shows me a sailboat and its reflection on the water, and says expectations are like reflections. It's a mistake to focus on a reflection and not on the actual fact. Expectations, like reflections, are never very clear. If you're focused on its reflection you can't see the actual sailboat, and you'll make mistaken assumptions. She says, 'It's great to use expectations to lay out goals, but withhold expectations of people so you can meet them where they are.' That will result in a better and easier way of communicating. She's talking about a particular person in your life. There is someone you're having a difficult time communicating with right now, a man."

"Oh, yes," said Aline.

"Make sure you're seeing him as he is now, and not only as he used to be. It will help your communication process."

"That's good to know," she answered. "I think I've been doing that because we've had such a rocky history. It's hard to see him in the present without looking through the filter of all that's happened in the past."

Is communication always easy? No way, especially if we got the message that our opinions or needs had no value. Speaking up without fearing reprisal is a common problem. As a hypnotist, I see clients who are hugely successful professionals, but who quake with fear at the thought of having to tell a spouse what they want. Many of my clients don't even know what they want, because they have been living someone else's dream or were molded by someone else's idea of what they should do. While spirit people don't express regret, they do acknowledge ways that they could have been happier or more peaceful when they were alive. Almost every one urges us to *know* ourselves, so we can *be* ourselves. From that solid platform, communication both ways is much easier.

Helpful Advice for Relationships

Later on in the same reading with Shelley, whose maternal grandfather cautioned about ignoring the elephant in the room, we received another valuable lesson. Her grandfather once again gave me the picture of lung cancer twice, so I knew he was stepping forward to offer another message. Usually multiple spirit people come through during readings, each with his own unique identifier or, as I envision it, his calling card. Once his message has been delivered, the spirit person will often stick around for the whole reading or circle. If he has a message to add to the conversation, he'll reintroduce himself by showing me his calling card. It's similar to a conference call, where none of the people are in the same room face-to-face. When someone wants to speak, he'll usually cut in and say, for example, "Jim here," and then proceed with his comment. Because I'm the only one in the reading with a direct line to the spirit people – or the only one who is using it at the time – the spirit person who wants to speak gives me his or her calling card. Shelley's grandfather gave me his calling card: the cancer ribbon with a numeral two over it accompanied by the impression of difficulty breathing. I knew he had more to say.

"He shows me a picture of railroad tracks going off into the distance, and how they appear to meet at the horizon," I said. "We know of course that railroad tracks never meet, and as we go on them and the horizon stays ahead of us, they appear to meet at the vanishing point. He shows me this and tells me some things in your life may never come together. I think he's talking about people or relationships – who may never come together or see eye-to-eye. They may never get along."

"I can see what he's talking about," Shelley offered.

"There's a relationship between parallels, even when they don't meet. I sense he's referring to a relationship about which people are saying, 'Oh, I wish they'd just get along!' He's saying, 'Instead of pretending that everything is smooth, pay attention to the reality and know that the relationship is acceptable even in the absence of total agreement.'"

"I should give up trying to get these two family members to get along?" Shelley asked.

"Running parallel is just as beneficial because the relationship is still there," I continued as her grandfather directed. "You don't always have to merge to have a relationship that's balanced. Your grandfather gives me the feeling he may have spent a lot of time wishing things were different or wishing everyone would just get along. Now he says that energy could have been used more to his benefit because it's okay if people don't see eye-to-eye. If you focus on the wish being unfulfilled all the time, you'll lose sight of the perfect balance that exists anyway. To flog this metaphor a little bit more, if you can appreciate your parallel tracks, you'll enjoy the illusion of working together, just as though you were walking along railroad tracks and seeing the illusion of the rails meeting."

Shelley acknowledged family members on her mother's side that didn't get along, and the anxiety it caused her grandfather for years before he passed.

"Now he says, 'Don't waste any time managing other people's feelings.' Let them have the relationships they're going to have with you or with others. Your responsibility is the direction you're going, and where other people are going is not your concern. If you try to make it your business, you're wasting a lot of time."

Many spirit people acknowledge disharmony in families they left behind, especially if they played a role in that. Shelley's maternal grandfather spent a long time concerned that members of his clan weren't getting along, and from the spirit world he was hoping to stop passing the torch of concern and urged his granddaughter to turn her energy to other things. It was a great comfort to her to learn that she didn't have to carry on her grandfather's tradition of trying to fix family squabbles. It was not his wish from beyond the grave that Shelley ensure her entire family see eye to eye. As Shelley exclaimed, "What a relief!"

***

In another reading my client Mel's mother came through, whom he was able to identify readily. The topic turned to Mel's sister after the spirit mother gave her message to Mel.

"She shows me you and your sister are like oil and water," I said.

Mel chuckled. "I guess you could say that."

"Not confrontation, but not mixing right. She's reflecting this back to you, and saying sometimes personalities are like oil and water, and you needn't blame anyone," I said.

"I keep trying to work on our relationship, but she's very

difficult," said Mel.

"Your mother tells me, 'The fault lies with neither the oil nor the water.' Sometimes things don't mix together. Appreciating the oil for its qualities and not trying to force it to mix well with water, or vice versa, is how everybody gets along. Don't put too much pressure on yourself to fix what may not naturally flow together anyway. Different elements combine differently and if two don't blend well it's not because one of the elements is wrong or deficient. This is normal in the natural world."

"Well, that's a relief," he said. "I'm not going to stop trying, but I'm not going to keep trying to force it."

***

At a message circle composed of people who'd worked together for years, I was drawn to give a message to a guest whose friend had come through from the spirit world. After being clearly identified by my guest, the spirit passed on a message about someone my guest worked with.

"She gives me the feeling of a co-worker being a snake in the grass, a cobra. My sense is this is not a dangerous person, but someone you are never going to see eye-to-eye with," I said.

"My friend wasn't like that!" my guest cried.

"No, she's talking about someone around you now, who is alive. She is talking about someone you work with," I said.

"No one here, though, right?" another guest joked.

"No, someone who isn't here tonight. She actually shows me a snake in the grass, and says sometimes it's better just to walk around these people. She shows this person as a reptile to highlight not so much the danger, but the inability to connect." Spirit people often show me a reptile to symbolize a relationship that isn't going to change in the way my client is hoping, or one which is unbalanced because one party is struggling to reach a common understanding and the other party cannot appreciate it.

"We can connect with mammals other than people because we're similar," I continued, "but reptiles don't have that type of brain. They have a primitive reptilian brain, and therefore don't have the ability to interact with us the way other creatures do, who have brains similar to our own," I said.

"Huh?" I explained why her friend used the reptile symbol.

"If you give a dog affection, it can process it and return affection because our brains are similar in that regard. If you give a snake affection, it doesn't read it as affection and bonding, and respond by giving affection back. If you try to have a cuddly bond with a lizard or snake, it's not going to happen because we're so far apart in our communication and connection possibilities, it's a waste of time. Do you see the comparison she is making?" I asked.

"I get it," my guest answered.

"She says you can respect this person's power or sneakiness. I don't feel as though this is out-and-out malice, I feel she has a singular agenda, or a singular, reptilian-brain way of looking at life. Better to say, 'Let me walk around you.' There may be a part of you that wants to keep reaching out or trying again, and your spirit friend says, 'Don't bother, because she won't be able to connect.' Even if you're giving one hundred percent, your co-worker isn't able to appreciate it. She's missing the more evolved part of the brain that gives us a social conscience. Not an evil person; just respect the different personality and walk around. Go on your own way."

"Okay."

"She doesn't believe you're listening!" I said, which made the others in the room laugh. "Your friend in spirit says you will not be rewarded, no matter how hard you try to get her to like you. This snake cannot relate to you. It's not your fault, it's not your failure if you don't get her to like you. She probably cannot like anyone."

This was a group of people I hadn't read before, and with each reiteration of the spirit person's point, I felt the tension grow. My guest looked slightly angry that I was telling her how to relate to a co-worker in a position of authority over her, and she argued with me about the importance of being in this person's good graces. Her friend in the spirit world, and even some of her co-workers who were present at the message circle, urged my guest not to let her worth be determined by the reflection of an authority figure who was fully focused on her own agenda. Sometimes I can see that messages from the spirit people hit home; other times such as this, I do what I can to deliver the message and then carry on. Neither I nor the spirit people are in the business of giving advice, and I frequently remind my clients they are under no obligation to follow the advice of a spirit person. It's not my responsibility to see that advice is followed, but I do try hard to see that the advice is at least heard.

***

Some time ago I was reading a man in a family group who had come for a circle. I was directed to him from a man in spirit who lost a son or who thought he lost a son. He came through with overwhelming grief at the loss of another male.

Speaking to Jim I said, "I have an older man in spirit who is deeply grieved by the loss of a son. I'm not sure if he means the son was literally lost, or their relationship was lost. He shows me Theseus returning without changing his sails from black to white."

"I don't know know what that means," Jim said. "My grandfather didn't have a good relationship with his son, but I don't know if that would be him. I don't know Theseus."

"The spirit people often use symbols to communicate a complex feeling," I said. "This man is showing me Theseus's father, from the Greek myth of the Minotaur. The short version is that against his father's wishes Theseus sailed on a ship with black sails to Crete, to kill the half-man/half-bull Minotaur. His father was the king of Athens and strongly opposed to his son's foolhardy plan. But Theseus assured him that he would kill the monster, and when he succeeded he would sail home with white sails on the ship instead of black ones. Theseus did kill the Minotaur, but on the return voyage he had to leave his fiancée with one of the gods who wanted her for himself, and in his sorrow Theseus forgot to change the sails from black to white. His father, who was watching the horizon, saw the ship with black sails returning and believed his son was dead. He was so overcome with grief, he threw himself off a cliff.

"Now this man in spirit," I continued, "he's talking about losing a son, literally, or he lost him in another way, and he never recovered from the grief of losing him. He gives me the feeling, 'I told my son what to do, to be safe, and he didn't listen, and I lost him.' He says, 'I tried to control this other life and I wasn't able to, and as a result I had a lot of grief.'

"That's definitely my grandfather," said Jim. "He's talking about my uncle. They didn't talk for about twenty years, and then my grandfather died."

"The bottom line is, 'Don't do what I did.' This is his message. Don't expect people to follow everything that you want them to do. The only thing that happens is you end up disappointed. He's commenting on you and what's going on in your mind right now when you ask yourself, 'What should I do with my life?'"

"Oh, my God!" cried Jim. "That's exactly what I've been asking myself, out loud, too, to all my friends! But I don't know how to answer that question."

"He wants to talk about controlling what you have control over and letting go of what you can't control," I said. "Your grandfather says, 'Live by your own values.' He suggests that to answer that question you first determine your own values. Find your top three values and pass relationships and work through this filter, as well as the life you lead. If they can't pass through, let them go."

"That's the biggest question," answered Jim. "I don't know what I want to do for a job."

"Instead of forcing a career into meeting the standards of how you want to live, stop the career. Do something different. If you don't, you live a life of continual disappointment. Instead of forcing a sweetheart to measure up to your standards, for instance, let her go. Otherwise, it's demoralizing for her and you end up disappointed in her all the time."

"That makes so much sense!" Jim replied. "I can't see why he would say that though, because he was completely the opposite."

"Spirit people have usually distilled a great wisdom out of their mistakes," I said to Jim. "Especially if they didn't live the life they're suggesting now in their messages. You better believe they finally figured out how they could have been happier!

"You want to be happy," I continued. "He says that the way to happiness and serenity is to determine what's important to you. What aligns with that, keep, and what doesn't align with it, let it go instead of trying to force it."

"That is the perfect formula for life," said Jim.

***

I have a regular phone client who lives in another state. We've been connecting for so long now, I almost feel that I know her spirit people as well as she did when they were alive. Yet during one phone reading in the not-too-distant past, Danielle's uncle and grandfather came through with the kind of wisdom that delights and surprises me.

Danielle had been challenged by relationships with her older teenaged children, and was worried that her uncle and grandfather were hanging back and not helping her as much as they had. After clearly establishing their identity, I said, "They're involved, but they're a little bit more remote. They're giving me the sense that you're handling things well. They're not away from you, but they're stepping back to watch you manage on your own. They're still connected with you."

"I don't feel like it, though," Danielle laughed. "I always used to hear them, or feel like I could go to sleep with a question for them and I'd wake up in the morning and know the answer. I'm not getting the answers the way I used to!"

"Your team is still there. We learn about our abilities when our teachers step back and allow us to try on our own. From time to time we have to test ourselves to make sure we understand the material before more learning can take place. They may have helped you more than you realize, and they're saying, 'Now's your chance to put what you've learned into action, and let's see how you go.' Your mother comes in now, too." I translated some particular things about Danielle's mother so that she was satisfied her mother in spirit had joined our conversation as well.

"Your mother is laughing, too, saying, 'You're getting it, you got it,'" I said.

"Oh, God," said Danielle, laughing. "How would she know?"

"She also says, 'Know that what you're doing is rewarded in Heaven, and don't waste too much time expecting reward here on earth.' If you get one, what a wonderful surprise, if you don't, you won't be disappointed," I said to Danielle. Her mother in spirit was laughing, though Danielle was upset. "She keeps saying, 'You got it!'"

"I'm not looking for a reward," said Danielle. "I'm looking for my children to work with and understand me. They walk all over me."

"Continue to take those actions or make those sacrifices that you feel are purposeful and rewarding. But don't sacrifice to make a point to your children. You'll end up feeling demoralized, confused, or indecisive, and that'll drain your energy, your finances, and your patience. Trust that your children will get it on their own. They may not get it till they're fifty-year-old parents themselves, when they're pulling their hair out saying, 'Mom, what do I do with this kid?' Then you'll be like your mother now in spirit, saying, 'You got it! You got it!'

"That 'I got it' comes for each of us in our own time," I continued translating the message from Danielle's spirit people. "You can teach your children things when they're small but like your uncle and grandfather, you have to step back and let them put what they learned into play. And if they don't get it, the consequences are theirs. They can come back to you and say, 'Look, I don't get this, can you help me,' or they'll muddle through or try and fail until they figure it out."

"I need to breathe and let it go," Danielle said.

"You might say to yourself, 'His reaction is not my concern.' Or, 'Her feelings are not my responsibility.' Continue to act in ways that are good for your family as a whole, regardless of how any one person might feel about it," I said. Danielle and I were both silent for a moment as that message sank in. I felt the spirit people impressing more of the message on me, so I continued.

"You feel happy because your family responds positively to your actions, but if they don't, you feel unhappy. Let your reason for happiness depend on taking those actions confidently, rather than on the response. You don't need to explain or defend yourself. To your husband perhaps, but certainly not to young children," I said.

"You're taking this information right out of my head!" Danielle laughed. "You're right, my daughter works for me and is always questioning me, and sometimes she is such a witch! 'How come you get to take time off? Where are you going?' And when I tell her, 'I don't have to answer to you,' it feels so good!"

"You can say that, or you can say, 'Because I feel like it,' and shrug your shoulders. It's coming out of my mouth but this is information your spirit people want me to say," I reminded her.

"Oh, I get that!" Danielle said.

"To the best of your ability, disengage from people's reactions. Yes, your daughter might kick and scream if you say, 'Because I want to,' and walk away ignoring her reaction. That is her issue. If she gets that feedback from several people, she's going to understand, 'Hey, maybe I'm being a witch, and if I want people to stay around me, I should probably think about the way I'm speaking.' But she's not going to hear that in words, according to your mother."

"She was the biggest witch of all, so she should know!" laughed Danielle.

"She also says that if you've been giving in forever, you can expect a lot of resistance when you start to change.

"It's difficult, for women in particular, to think we might make someone unhappy with the choices we make. Your mother shows me that if anyone reacts with less than one hundred percent support for you, you shrink back. You try to explain your reasons, defend your decisions, or you get into a fight because you feel threatened somehow. It's hard to be okay with silence or a negative reaction, but you don't have step in and manage that reaction. You don't need to make sure people are happy. Your mother says, 'I was spending a lot of time making sure everyone around me was okay with my decisions, and that's not necessary.' It's a hard thing to change."

"Yes, it is," Danielle said. "And my mother became so resentful and critical because she did what everyone else wanted her to do, and then she got mad because nobody would help her do what she wanted to do."

I let a moment of silence go by.

"Oh, my God!" Danielle laughed out loud. "I could be talking about myself, exactly!"

"Once you begin to change it, it is quite liberating," I replied, as I continued to share her spirit mother's impressions. "No one can argue with, 'I felt like it.' The other person can hold his breath until he turns blue in the face, but don't diminish your experience in life or abandon yourself so he doesn't have to deal with his insecurities. The chips are going to fall where they may, and it's not your concern to make sure that everybody is happy with your tone of voice and the way that you're speaking. You can't do that anymore."

"I'm going to listen to this recording every night before I go to bed!" said Danielle.

"Your mother says, 'You're this close to happiness and contentment. If you'd just get out of your own damn way!'"

"She should know," said Danielle. "Well, I guess she knows now, because she didn't know that when she was alive."

"Spirit people always tell me, 'Things will all make sense when you're dead,'" I replied.

Danielle's mother gave her advice that she herself was unable to appreciate when alive in the physical body. In the afterlife she could clearly see that her relationship missteps came from a specific behavior that Danielle appeared to be repeating. Hoping to steer her away from resentment and towards joy, she playfully used herself as an example of how not to relate to children.

***

I did a phone reading with another woman who was in anguish over her children also, but for a different reason, and this time it was a mother-in-law in spirit who came in with advice.

"I am the one who separated my children from their dad," Bonnie said, "and I feel so guilty about that." We had just begun our reading when my client blurted this out. She wanted to know if her loved ones in spirit judged her, especially her former mother-in-law, with whom she had been close before her death. After connecting with the mother-in-law in spirit, whom Bonnie was able to validate through the various bits of evidence the spirit offered, I began to translate the message. It was in direct response to Bonnie's concern about her children.

"Your mother-in-law says your children are just fine. You're the gateway through which they came into the world. They are a product of you biologically, you and their dad, but they are their own people, with their own spirits. They chose to come through to you at this time, and if you think about it this way, you just created the doorway through which they came into the world. They're going to be exactly who they are. They're fully formed spiritually, and they're brilliant and perfect."

"I forgot that. I forgot that we choose our parents," said Bonnie. She explained that before getting married and having children she had explored different spiritual traditions. That search had opened her eyes to many ideas that subsequently resonated with her.

"Keep reminding yourself of that, because your children have as much to teach you as you have to teach them," I continued, as her mother-in-law impressed her message on me. "So if you respect them, and I know that you do, remind yourself that they're actually a lot closer to innocence and perfection because they haven't been around long enough to get jaded. They are able to remind you, 'Hey, I'm already perfect,' so that you can start looking at yourself the same way. 'They chose to come in at this time, we all made this arrangement before we were even born. Don't blame yourself.'"

"I haven't screwed them up?" Bonnie asked hopefully.

"Your mother-in-law says you haven't screwed them up," I said. "They're already perfectly formed spiritually. Your job is to let them know that they're safe and to remind them that they're lovable and everything else is in God's hands, and that will affirm their healthy emotional, mental, and physical formation. That's how to relate to them no matter what's going on between you and their dad. If they don't see you beating yourself up or feeling guilty about things, then they won't assume there's anything to feel guilty about."

"That's brilliant," said Bonnie.

"Yes, it is!" I replied. "I wish I could take credit for it! If there's nothing to feel guilty about, they'll be as trusting and easy-going about love as when we all come into the world. Love has no beginning and no end. And just because relationships end it doesn't mean that love stops. You don't have to feel guilt when you look at them."

"I knew she would calm me down," said Bonnie. "She was more like my mother than my mother-in-law, and she was always telling me to relax and not worry so much. I guess she still is!"

***

In one last example of the spirits' view of relationships, I'd like to share part of a poignant reading for a retirement-age client of mine. I don't often have men come for one-on-one readings, so it's always a pleasant surprise. Men bring a totally different energy to the meeting than women do, maybe in part because men have been taught not to cry or show too much emotion. When things get emotional my male clients sometimes deflect the message or deny the connection. More often than not however, the spirit people nudge past these barriers with consistent, undeniable evidence; I discreetly place the tissue box on the table between us and carry on. Sometimes my male clients get so uncomfortable or are so resistant that they aren't able to acknowledge any information that comes through. You'd be surprised to learn that some people make appointments, pay my fee, and then refuse to acknowledge or listen to the messages from their loved ones. Even if another person in the room is saying, "That's Dad! You know he said that!" some folks are just resistant to the experience.

Don's wife had been to see me in a group of her friends for a message circle, and at a later date for a one-on-one reading. She thought her husband would love an appointment so she made one for him. When Don showed up we shook hands, sat down, and got right to work. After about ten minutes I handed Don his money back and showed him to the door. I can't imagine why he'd agreed to come in the first place.

"There's a woman in spirit here who shows me her name is Lily or Lila," I said to Don, within a few seconds of tuning in to my sixth sense. "She's the grandmother. Tiny. She wasn't born in this country but came here as a girl with her father. Her mother stayed in Europe with the younger children and came here later. Do you know who this is?" I asked.

"Maybe," said he.

"Okay," I said. I waited, but the grandmother in spirit just fed me the same information again. "Do you have a grandmother with the name Lily or Lila?"

"Hmm," Don said, neutrally. Let me mention that I hadn't met this spirit person when Don's wife had been to see me. Because I never want to use my memory during readings, I ask spirit people whom I may have met before to give me a totally different way to present them if another family member or even the original one returns for a subsequent reading with me.

I could tell by now that Don wasn't going to participate much at all in this session. With that in mind, I asked the grandmother to show me an activity Don had done that very day. Something unique that she observed; something to which he would have to respond either "yes" or "no."

"She shows me you ate chicken wings for breakfast," I said to Don. "I'm not talking about wings you would get at a fast food restaurant, but an actual leftover chicken wing that was in your refrigerator."

Don didn't say anything.

"Does this make sense?" I asked him. "Did you eat chicken wings for breakfast?"

"I don't know," said Don.

"Okay, look," I said. "This question has no grey area, it's a 'yes' or 'no' question. You either ate wings for breakfast or you didn't."

"Yes," Don admitted.

We carried on in this fashion for another five minutes before I invited Don to take his money back and go on about his day, which he did. As I do at the end of every appointment, I emailed him the ten minute recording of our reading. When his wife listened to it she called me and acknowledged for him all the details he wouldn't acknowledge himself. I saw Don's wife recently and we laughed about this all over again.

***

When septuagenarian Jimmy came to my door I was looking forward to connecting him with his loved ones in the spirit world and wondering just how accepting he would be.

"I have a man here in spirit who passed a long, long time ago," I began. "In the late sixties, I believe. This is a young man, late teens, he shows me nineteen."

"Boy, that's hard to remember," Jimmy replied.

"Okay," I said, "I'm going to give you more. He shows me the face of a singer who was popular when I was young, named Bobby Sherman. This young man may have the name Bobby or Sherman." I explained to Jimmy that being primarily clairvoyant (seeing in my mind's eye) and clairsentient (feeling mental and physical impressions), I didn't hear names clearly. Because of this the spirit people would show me the face of someone else I might recognize – usually a saint because of my Catholic upbringing, but sometimes a celebrity or even a friend or family member of my own.

"This man drank a lot," I continued. "This man was in combat, he shows me Viet Nam."

"Oh! Wait a minute!" said Jimmy.

"He was so cool," I went on. "He had lots of pretty girls on the back of his motorcycle. He drank himself to death after coming back from the Viet Nam War."

"I know him," said Jimmy, with wonder in his voice. "That was my best friend's older brother. He was just like you said. We all wanted to be like him."

"Here's his message," I said. "When a spirit person gives me an impression, he may be talking about himself or talking about you. Usually he's talking about his experience, and turning it into a message for you. Such as, 'Do what I did,' or, 'Don't do what I did.'"

"Okay," Jimmy said.

"He says, 'Take the boxing gloves off.' Don't look for conflict where there isn't one. You don't have to butt heads. Resolve conflicts, life is short. Let go of a relationship with someone you don't get along with – not the relationship, but the conflict in the relationship. Be the bigger person. Just say, 'I'm not going to fight about this anymore.' Step out of the way and let punches go by you. You don't always need to have a conflict."

"I know what he means," Jimmy replied.

"One person can say, 'I'm not going to have a conflict anymore.' Conflict can't continue if one of the parties doesn't engage. He says, 'When I was alive, I was great, but I couldn't step out of the conflict and my whole life went down the tubes.' If one perpetuates conflict, it only ends up destroying oneself, and not serving any purpose."

After Bobby's message, Jimmy told me that he was struggling in a conflict-wrought relationship, where he felt it was important to be right and not give in. He acknowledged that he often faced the world with boxing gloves on, always expecting confrontation and conflict.

Before I discovered the power of self-hypnosis and the spiritual tradition I follow today, I spent hours talking to therapists about my difficult experiences and other perceived shortcomings, just as many people do. I was overly concerned about how others saw me, whether I was living up to expectations, and feeling guilt and anxiety about my relationships. The spirit people were just like us when they were in their physical bodies, and they struggled with many of the same worries and fears. Once in the Heavenly realm, they've been able to see what is truly valuable in physical life, which is to love and accept ourselves just as we are, to recognize that our spirits are not broken, and to turn our attention and energy to pursuing our own fulfillment. Relationships and children are the perfect mirrors to reflect our progress, and give us honest feedback about how well we are doing on our road to self-realization. So often we get side-tracked into fixing the other person or the relationship itself, while our loved ones in the spirit world encourage us to put our energy into what we can change, the source – ourselves.

Self Regard and Personal Power

A spirit came through who was identified easily by my client Ellen, as her mother's close friend Gail. The spirit woman mentioned attending a family baptism in the near future, which Ellen acknowledged. As spirit people often do, Gail used this identifier first as evidence of her connection to Ellen, then as a symbol around which to craft her message.

"Gail wants me to tell you that it is never too late to wash yourself clean of who you were in the past so you can be re-born," I said. "She is not specifically talking about a religious rite here. She's talking about forgiveness and forgiveness of oneself in particular. Let go of old grudges or wounds, wash your heart and your spirit clean. She says, 'It's never too late to do that.' I'm not talking about accepting childhood abuse, but that we can cleanse our minds and hearts from the pain, and keep the factual data so it doesn't happen again. She's using the sacrament of baptism to say, 'Be born again. Start again.' Obviously you can't be born again to new parents as an adult, but you can decide to have a different view of your childhood."

Ellen hadn't said a word during this message, though I could feel her watching me closely.

"She's talking about emotional baggage; you're highly critical of yourself. There's a voice from your childhood saying, 'Oh, you can't do that, you're not smart enough.' Gail says tune that voice out and recreate the part of your childhood that the voice affected. Create a sense of yourself that is hopeful, optimistic, positive, and adventurous: What's going to happen tomorrow? What will I learn this afternoon? Gail says that's the best outlook on life, where you believe you're worthy of love, a good person, and it's okay if you make mistakes. You have every right to be here. 'Just because you *make* mistakes doesn't mean you *are* a mistake.' That's what she's talking about."

Ellen admitted that she struggled with low self-esteem and always questioned her value in a family where she was routinely criticized.

"When you go to the upcoming family baptism, release your self-judgment or anyone else's judgment that you might have taken on. Wash it away when you take a shower," I said. "Gail says, 'Remind yourself that all of your needs are valid.' You're entitled to have them, even if your needs aren't always met. Spirits come into the world with a wonderful, open-ended optimism about the life unfolding for them. Endeavor to have that view of yourself, too."

Gail was encouraging my client to outgrow erroneous voices from her childhood that had kept her locked in a cycle of self-judgment, self-criticism, and low regard for her own personhood in the world. By suggesting Ellen recreate a religious ritual in the simple act of showering, Gail hoped to help Ellen see herself the way little children see themselves: as worthy of attention, love, and care.

We're all entitled to feel empowered and in control of our lives, but the avenues to personal power can be tricky to navigate. Most often because we don't recognize that we've misplaced or given away our power.

***

On the phone with my regular client Clarice, we were forty-five minutes into our hour-long session before she mentioned how overwhelmed she was feeling, and how powerless to create any change in her life. Many of her loved ones in spirit had already been giving messages, but at this remark they surged forward collectively to give Clarice the following advice.

"Though I'm only getting one signal, they're all sending this message to you," I said. "Your spirit people are showing me Sampson and Delilah from the Old Testament story."

"Oh, I know that story," said Clarice.

"The secret to Samson's great strength was that he had never cut his hair. Delilah seduces him so he'll reveal his weakness. One night after she sleeps with him she cuts off his hair and betrays him. His enemies throw him into prison, and he can't resist because now he's weak. But eventually his hair grows back, and he destroys his captors. Your spirit people are showing me this whole story and telling me that you need to let some time pass, let your hair grow out, so to speak. Your feelings of power will come back. You may have been seduced by self-expectations or people's expectations of you. Not a literal seduction, but you believe you have to make a great change or solve a problem, and it's flummoxed you.

"Understand the difference between *awareness* of your power, and the *fact* of your power. You only *think* you are powerless, and that perception renders you so. In truth you are not and never have been. If you can separate yourself from the feeling of powerlessness, it will be just a short time before your hair grows back and you remember that your power has always been within you." I was truly pleased to be delivering this message. The spirit people frequently use Bible stories or myths as analogies. Being raised a Catholic first, and being taught to love literature second, I have a mental library full of stories. Spirit people are aware of this, and they browse in the library of my mind until they find the tale that most closely matches their message. When they do, they pull it off the shelf, hand it to me and say, "Here, tell this one." I hadn't thought of the Samson and Delilah story in more years than I can remember, but Clarice knew it as well as I did. I said, "This is a good one, I've never had the spirit people use this story before."

"I looked at their pictures before our call," said Clarice of her family members in spirit. "I asked for my grandmother, but I didn't know they'd all come. I'm so happy, I'm crying."

"Because they keep showing me Delilah, they're talking about the things of the world that are seductive," I said. "They're not talking about women being the problem, or religion as the answer, though."

"I know exactly what they mean," she said. Clarice knew her real power lay in understanding where her *only* power lay – in her ability to choose how she would respond. She admitted to being drawn into the false belief that power came with accomplishment, rising up through the corporate ranks, earning money, or being influential. She allowed external circumstances to overwhelm her. Her spirit people encouraged Clarice to find peace by studying what had seduced her and understanding the power she had unwittingly given up.

We find enormous strength in our own intuition, too, if we learn to trust in it. Every single person has a sixth sense, but we often dismiss its signal if it doesn't coincide with data from the five senses. Trusting your intuition – and letting it add to your good judgment – elevates your powers of discernment so that you never second-guess yourself again, or miss so-called red flags, or make decisions you later regret. Trusting your gut feelings is as empowering as knowing that the only thing under your control, ever, is how you choose to react.

***

My client Linda was with me for her yearly birthday reading. When her grandmother came in with unique identifiers, Linda was able to validate her presence right away.

"Your grandmother shows me an old well pump," I said. "I see something in you that you have to draw up. It's in there, this life-giving, refreshing, satisfying, necessary part of being alive. No, she's correcting me," I interrupted myself. Interruptions are a fairly regular occurrence in readings, and I appreciate the precision spirit people demand of me in translating their messages. Linda's grandmother had given me a feeling, and as I began to process it through the unavoidable filter of my conscious mind, I'd apparently put my own spin on it. I'd extrapolated beyond her intended meaning. The grandmother in spirit immediately stopped delivering the message to me, which feels similar to forgetting what I was about to say. If you've ever opened your mouth to speak and drawn a complete blank, you'll understand the feeling. It's a similar to forgetting someone's name, or as though the ground beneath me just disappeared, leaving me feeling rather foolish. What was there a moment ago is now empty space. Linda's grandmother was pretty gentle with her correction, though sometimes interruptions feel more like a firm smack on the head. I waited for Linda's grandmother to fill the empty space with her correction.

"Are you following a more intuitive path now? More meditative?" I asked.

"Yes, that's happening," says Linda.

"You're going to be drawing on this and getting stronger," I said.

"Why did she want to correct you?" Linda asked me.

"I was getting the impression that you were going to have to pump this up to the surface, and she said, 'No.' This is more like a modern day well where you turn the tap on and water comes out."

"I used to work so hard at my intuition, and now it seems to be coming easily and naturally."

"How is that working out for you?" I asked her.

"It's amazing how calm I feel," she answered. "I don't agonize over the business anymore. Life seems much easier. I feel as though I can't make any wrong steps, and that has built my confidence enormously."

Her grandmother wanted to draw attention to Linda's inherent intuition so that she could grow in confidence and empowerment. By pointing out to Linda that she saw her accessing that valuable flow of information, her grandmother in spirit was connecting deeply to Linda and encouraging her trust in the sixth sense.

It's interesting how Linda had been working hard to make her intuition more present in her life without experiencing much success. This hard work could be counterproductive, especially if one is trying to bend the sixth sense experience into information that satisfies the rational mind. When we think of hard work, that usually means we have to focus on a subject, figure it out logically, and measure results. That model works well if you're trying to learn a new skill, save money for a better car, or strategize how to improve your relationship. If ever you have a desire to increase the flow of ideas or data from the sixth sense, it's a good idea to practice not-doing rather than doing. It's more important to become familiar with what your intuition feels like – *for you* – and begin to get comfortable with fitting those sensations into your everyday experience. At the end of this section, you'll find a meditation to help you work less hard at getting to know that important voice, while enjoying more success.

***

Agatha came for a one-on-one reading with me and was immediately greeted by her friend Gina in the spirit world. After giving evidence of her identity, Gina addressed some of the questions Agatha had with a simple message about not-doing.

"She's creating a picture," I said as I waited for the subtle images in my mind's eye to settle into an impression I could translate. "It's a puzzle; she's going to make a message out of it. You work on a jigsaw puzzle, and sometimes you can't find a piece though you search and search. Then other times you simply walk by the table where the puzzle is and you see the piece and put it right in place. It just seems to jump out because you're not looking for it. Gina says, 'Your picture is forming,'" I said to Agatha.

"Well, sometimes I think so," Agatha said, "but then there's nothing there."

"You don't want it to be finished yet, so there is no need to hurry. Working hard at it can be frustrating. Sometimes you just walk by and put the piece in. The full picture forms. She shows me the old game show with Vanna White, the one with the letters. Do you know what I mean?" I asked.

"Wheel of Fortune?" asked Agatha.

"Yes!" I said. "She shows me a picture of words with letters missing. We can rack our brains, stare right at it, and get nothing. But then we look at it again and we just get it. Set a task to your subconscious mind and it will get done more quickly than if you use your conscious mind."

Agatha admitted she had been trying – and trying, and trying – to trust her intuition in her business and spiritual growth. Her friend in the spirit world wanted Agatha to see that achieving what she hoped for was more in the awareness of what was already present, than in the specific creation or the pursuit of it with her logical mind.

Balance and Martyrdom

One theme the spirit people repeatedly touch on concerns balance. We sometimes may mistake overemphasis on our own perceived importance for genuine empowerment, and the spirits like to remind us that exerting massive amounts of energy to prop up a perception is a waste of our resources. If we focus on how to fix others, fix relationships, or otherwise create drama, we're missing opportunities to understand how easily we can achieve and maintain balance. We could give energy to the things that are under our control.

My client Billie's mother came through during our private reading. After Billie identified her, the mother passed on an unusual message.

"She has a concern that you are martyring yourself for a cause," I said. "I don't know why she shows me this. She shows me a figure putting herself up on a cross. She's describing herself, but she's directing this towards you." Spirit people often begin their messages by showing an identifiable characteristic about themselves, and then expanding it into a lesson or suggestion.

"Well..." she drawled out, rather noncommittally.

"Your mother says, 'Nobody celebrates a martyr until after she's gone.' You might want to scale back the power you're giving away. The recipients don't value it." Knowing there was more to come from her mother, I waited a moment.

"If you're doing it for yourself and you feel rewarded by it, that's fine. But the extra effort that you're giving may not be noticed," I said. "She shows me that's because people may not be able to absorb the extra energy that you're giving; as a result you may be going into a deficit. Another way to say this is the people you're doing things for can only receive a certain amount, and then they cannot show you their appreciation for all the extra you're doing. Then it seems to you that they don't appreciate *anything* you're doing, so you then do even more. Similar to a glass that cannot hold any more water, yet you keep pouring it anyway and blame the glass for not being able to take all you're giving. She's saying, 'Nobody notices how great you are for doing that until after you're gone.' Scale that effort back and it won't make a difference to those who are on the receiving end," I continued. Still not sure I'd translated that correctly, I paused once again.

"If the giving is for you, that's one thing," I told Billie. "If your great joy comes from giving above and beyond your means to give, that's one thing. But if you're giving at a level where you are hoping to positively influence someone's life, take note, because a person can only fill up to a set point and then anything beyond that won't be noticed."

"I get it," said Billie.

"When they're away or you're long gone, that's when they'll say, 'Oh, Billie was wonderful.' But you want to be appreciated in your own time. If you scale back overgiving, nobody will be worse for it and you would feel better," I said. "Was your mother a martyr?"

"Oh, yes," Billie answered.

"So there it is straight from the horse's mouth. Nobody notices until you're gone," I finished. We talked a bit more about Billie's emotional and physical fatigue from overextending herself, and how frustrated she felt when no one appreciated her. Understanding from her mother – who knew from her own personal experience – that overgiving is like trying to add more water to a glass that's already full, Billie vowed to step back and think about what was motivating her to overgive. This was preferable to focusing on why those she gave to weren't as appreciative as she expected them to be, or why their level of gratitude did not match the level of her effort.

***

My client Natalie had a visit from her grandmother in spirit during a message circle I held in another state. After identifying herself and being validated by Natalie, the grandmother described a life of helpless imbalance. She told us how she had invested all of her love and affection in one son, the one she felt had the most promise.

"Does this sound like your grandmother?" I asked Natalie, after describing this particular trait.

"From the stories my mother told me, yes, it does," she answered.

"But he died," I said. "She shows me she put all her eggs in this basket, but then the son died, and she had nothing else. She was bitter after this, and mad at God."

"Yes, my uncle died in his early twenties," Natalie told me.

"She wants to say something specific to you," I replied. "She is using her own example and shaping it into a message. She says, 'Make sure that the important things in your life get equal time, so that you can stay in balance.' Many people forget this. If one leg of a three-legged stool is shorter or weaker than the others, then things start to get unstable. We're out of balance, and we have to cut down one leg and then another, until before we know it we're on the floor."

"That is exactly what I need to hear!" claimed Natalie. "I wouldn't have put myself in the same category as she, with just loving one of her children, but I can see that I'm doing the same thing. I've been completely out of balance lately," she continued, "and I've just been complaining about it but I haven't been able to change it."

"I like the picture she shows me of the stool," I said. "It's a great symbol of how weakness in one area can affect the overall balance."

Natalie's grandmother saw an opportunity to coach her granddaughter in the equal distribution of resources. Giving equal time to important efforts – herself included – was the most efficient way to a life of balance.

***

One young man came in from the spirit world to refine a message about balance for my client Avril. She recognized him as a friend from college. His own personal recklessness had lead to his passing, and as spirits usually do when they want to make this claim, he held up his hand in a sheepish wave.

"When a spirit holds up his hand like this," I said, "he means to say, 'My actions lead to my passing.' He's not talking about suicide, but that his decisions got him into a pickle."

"He was going too fast, and speed was the cause of his accident," she replied.

"He's trying to talk about how alive he felt," I said. "Well, no, that's not it. He's talking about how a person feels alive, and he's matching this feeling with you."

"I feel alive!" Avril joked.

"When we begin something enjoyable, we feel excited, vibrant, more alive," I continued. "He's talking about a heightened sense of awareness and wants you to be careful not to muddy that. He shows me you're starting a new business," I said.

"Yes, I just told my boyfriend I want to start a new business," Avril replied.

"All of your senses are heightened by newness, and your friend advises against dulling that sensitivity with too much food or drink, or arguing. He's suggesting you extend the 'high' of newness by cutting down on alcohol and keeping your body and mind as clear as possible. Celebrate with things that don't cloud your enthusiasm. Of himself he says, 'I didn't do the right thing with my own vibrant energy. I made poor choices and ended up where I am – dead.' Keep as clear as possible. As that 'high' builds and grows, it's going to attract more reasons to feel that vitality."

By suggesting that Avril adjust her quite reasonable alcohol intake to even less, her friend was showing her how to extend the fresh excitement of her new business. He wisely illustrated how balance requires flexibility, and how necessary it is to make minor adjustments as new opportunities and ideas arise. In all of these examples, the spirit people encourage us to be light on our feet, spontaneous, and flexible, because the achievement and maintenance of balance require near-constant shifting, sometimes in subtle ways and other times in major areas.

Your Destiny and Finding Yourself

In the ongoing work of staying in balance, we feel called to seek ourselves, our destinies, or our purpose in new ways. We answer this call by reinventing ourselves after the end of a relationship; changing careers after specializing in one field for years; or, finally pursuing a dream after retirement.

My client Maggie was concerned about the future of her sweetheart D.J., who was graduating from school with neither direction nor plan for his future. All she knew was that he was leaving their relationship, and she was understandably upset. When her spirit people came through for us, she asked if she could do more to keep him close or to bring him back. Her mother, whom she was quickly identified, answered first.

"She shows me in the near- to mid-term future that D.J. is moving," I said to Maggie. "Moving around, both geographically and in his dreams. I have a picture of him trying on several different 'lives' as he gets to know himself as a man. He's unsettled, in part because his dreams don't quite match his abilities and resources, but I suspect this is common for young men. Your mother tells me that's what 'finding yourself' means – to have dreams that are within reach, and to develop the discipline and personal resources to pursue them."

Part of Maggie's distress originated in not knowing what *she* was going to do next, now that D.J. was moving away. Having pinned much of her plans on a future with him, Maggie's need to find her own way suddenly moved to the top of the list. For Maggie, finding herself meant discovering her own desires, purpose, and destiny.

***

Taylor was able to validate both her father and grandfather during a message circle with her co-workers.

"Your grandfather wants to speak about about destiny. He's talking about genes, DNA," I said. "A run of bad luck is not in one's genes. Having a rough start in life is not predestination. Struggling is not destiny."

"I'm not sure I understand yet," said Taylor.

"He says, 'You don't have it,'" I continued. "Let me be more specific. Both your father and grandfather are encouraging you to imagine that your person – your cells, body, and spirit – are brand new every day. You're not carrying anything from the previous generations. Did one of these guys have a rough life or a rough start?" I asked.

"Yes, they both did," said Taylor.

"Okay, that's why they're using their own example to create this message to you," I said. "Their rough start – something about their history – doesn't have to define you. It's not programmed in you, that's what they're telling me. These two spirit men are encouraging you to think of every day as a fresh start. If you seem to be repeating a pattern that has happened in previous generations, they're discouraging you from giving it too much attention. Don't give too much time to the rough patches and recognize that your spirit is completely untainted by your genetics." I waited as both grandfather and father impressed me with the next thought.

"I don't know why they would say this," I said, "But I'm hearing, 'There's nothing wrong with you.' Everything about you is brand new, and there's nothing that you automatically have to overcome. Every day going forward they see you getting brighter. Both spirits see you struggling, and at the same time they're showing me that your light is reaching farther. The result isn't that you are getting better as a person, but that your self-perception of damage is falling away."

Taylor was wiping her eyes when I looked up at her, and a few of her co-workers were looking at her with quiet interest.

"Struggling is not your destiny," I concluded. "Your destiny is in a subtle self-correction that simply recognizes that you're already perfect, no damage needs to be corrected."

After our circle was over, Taylor phoned me to fill in some of the details she didn't feel comfortable validating in front of her co-workers. She admitted that she struggled with alcohol, as both her father and grandfather had. She had been so concerned that she had the "alcoholic gene," that the notion itself was crippling. If this was her destiny, why bother fighting it? With encouragement from those who now knew better, Taylor recommitted to seeing herself as someone with infinite possibility, not someone whose destiny was inescapably written in her DNA. We met on several occasions after that, for the purpose of teaching self-hypnosis and giving Taylor the tools to discover her strengths and pursue her dreams.

One of the challenges she faced was changing the dynamic in her family. Those who had invested emotionally in Taylor had been disappointed repeatedly and now no one trusted her. Offered hope and encouragement by her spirit father and grandfather, Taylor herself took up the reins of her destiny. I'm happy to say that she stopped drinking and is attending school part time to finish her degree; Taylor knows she can bring all of her ideas to life and confidently works towards that end.

***

While I was finishing this section of the book, a young woman named Donna attended a message circle with a few of her friends.

"I have a man here who shows me a stethoscope," I began. "This is a symbol that he was in the medical field. He also shows me wings – was he a pilot, or did he fly for the Red Cross?" I asked.

"I don't think I know him," Donna said.

"Yes, he says, 'Yes, you do,'" I laughed. "'It's no use denying it,' he says. He stands next to your father [whom we had already identified and heard a message from]. He's a friend of your father's. He shows me flying, and the medical profession."

"Oh, wait!" Donna said. "Now I know who he is! He volunteered for Doctors Without Borders or one of those organizations where you fly around to poorer parts of the world and volunteer to help people."

"I don't know what he means by this, so I'm just going to say it," I said. "He shows me an old Singer sewing machine."

"His last name was Singer," Donna said.

"Okay, that explains it," I said. "My mother had an old sewing machine like that when I was a girl. I don't sew at all so I wouldn't recognize a more modern one. That explains why he showed me the vintage model.

"Dr. Singer is talking about an idea. He shows that mushrooms grow in the dark. Goals or ideas sometimes thrive when they're not brought out into the light until they're ready to be shared."

"Oh boy, I know what he means!" said Donna, eyes gleaming.

"He is offering advice, though you don't need to take it," I reminded her. "Let your new idea develop deeper roots before sharing it with other people, otherwise you might be discouraged from pursuing it."

"I know what he means," said Donna, "but is he telling you something specifically?"

"He shows me an idea you have about bringing two unusual things together, two things that might otherwise seem like they don't belong.

You're inventing something!" I said.

"Well, I'm trying to," Donna replied. "Should I tell you what it is?"

"No!" I answered her. "Don't give me any information about it. The doctor says the time will come when it's strong enough to put out there, and no matter what anyone says you won't feel you have to go back and re-think it. People have an expectation of you. If you reveal this idea early, someone in your life will discourage you."

"People have an expectation of you. If you reveal this idea early, someone in your life will discourage it or stamp it down."

"I'm worried about that," she concurred.

"Dr. Singer suggests you keep it close to the vest, keep it inside while you work out the details. Many forces are at play; several spirit people and other guides want to see this invention come into the world," I said.

"I feel like it's my destiny to create a huge impact on the world," said Donna.

"That may be so," I answered. "Others may not see your destiny that way, and may be uncomfortable if you outshine them. Keep that in mind when considering who to share your ideas with."

Donna relayed to me after the circle that a few members of her family regularly discouraged her from pursuing new ideas. Her father had been one among them when he was alive. He wanted all of his children to "dream small," so they wouldn't know disappointment. It was interesting that he had his good friend Dr. Singer impart this particular message to Donna. Maybe he understood that she wouldn't believe it valid coming from him.

Donna received a relevant and practical message. As long as she keeps her hands on the reins of her own destiny, her creative drive to invent just may change the world.

Resolving Problems

I don't usually bring spirit guides into a reading unless the client specifically asks me to. As a medium, I consider my work to be connecting my clients with loved ones in the afterlife; I want to bring in spirits that the physical people can positively identify. If we all realize we'll be together again in love and peace, we can set aside fear and all the behaviors that arise out of fear. That includes judgment, guilt, worry, low self-esteem, feelings of isolation or loneliness, intolerance, prejudice, and even extends into criminal behavior such as robbery or murder.

Some of my regular clients are already assured that their loved ones in the spirit world are safe, happy, and forgiven. They'll ask me to tune into other beings, guides, or teachers who might be available to help them.

Judith is one of these clients. She explores many different faiths and practices meditation regularly. She is learning to trust her own intuitive guidance, and wanted an appointment to see if she could identify a certain spirit guide. We agreed that a light state of hypnosis would quiet the interfering rational mind and enhance her subconscious connection. After inducing the hypnotic trance, I asked Judith to keep her challenge in mind, and stay alert to any sensation of approach.

"Someone is here who looks like Buddha," she said.

"What does he say?" I asked her.

"Buddha says I'm not looking at it the right away," she answered.

"You're not looking at the problem the right way?" I asked.

"That's the question; that is what I should be analyzing," Judith replied. "He tells me that's what I have to think about – how am I looking at things. And then my answer will be clear. I'm not looking at it the right way. The challenge for me is not so much to make a decision, but how to look at it."

"Can he show you how to do that?" I prompted.

After a few moments, Judith answered. "I see a lot of sleeping people. They look like a whole bunch sarcophagi. They are all these sleeping saints. This is a trick. I have to go past this."

"Keep going," I said. "Tell me what you see next."

"Here's a guide that I recognize," Judith laughed. "I have a bone to pick with you!"

"Who is this?" I asked her.

"He looks like a monk," she said. "He shows up from time to time with others in a circle around me in my meditation. He's here alone this time. He says, 'Make the simplest choice.' He says it's not that easy. Part of me is guarding a secret very closely."

"Is that right?"

"No: There's a secret part of me that is guarded closely. That's what I mean. I don't understand this. He's talking about a secret that, once revealed, will alter my perception. A part of me, once understood, will change the way I see things. But he's not telling me how to access this part of me. He says, 'That's the challenge. That's the reason that I'm here, and why we're all here.' It's the same thing that Buddha said: I'm not looking at this the right way. Once I look at it the right way, this won't even be a decision. When I access this secret – as yet undiscovered, that's what I mean. When I get to this as-yet-undiscovered part of me, then a decision won't be necessary. And I'm asking him, 'How do I do that?' and he says, 'That's the job you have to do. That's just it.'

"Could you ask him if this involves a third party? Another person?" I asked.

"No. He's telling me, this which is consuming my life right now is not the real question. And if I look at the real question, then this challenge will resolve itself. I have to think about this. He's not going to tell me the answer, but says I have to pray for, or meditate on the question: 'How can I look at this differently?' Something will be revealed or understood then. These questions will be small and easily answered. I'm consumed with a splinter on the tip of a finger when I should be looking at the heart beating in the torso."

"Do you sense anything in the circumstances of life unfolding outside of you that will make things clear for you? Something that you don't have control over at this point?"

"No, I have control over this," she said. "I've been asking and praying for the wrong thing. If I turn my attention to the right question to ask then I'm looking for the disease instead of the symptom. It's positive, I don't mean to use a negative example. I've been addressing the symptom and not seeing where the real resolution lies. He's talking about the Holy Spirit. I need to familiarize myself with this power. Because even if I ask God, I couldn't understand the resolution without the help of an intercessor. If I ask the Holy Spirit to show me what I should be looking at, I will understand where I'm going."

"Can you do this now, in this session?" I asked.

"I have to pray for a shift in my perception," she said. "And this is the work. This is what they're telling me – this is the human being. Rather than praying for a resolution to my problems I should pray for a shift in my perception. I will see that I have no problems. This is as far as I can go, I'm sure, at this time."

Both of us were rather astonished at this clear direction for the resolution of problems.

Life Is Never Wasted

In one message circle a young man came through for my guest. He had passed away during the commission of a petty crime involving drugs.

"He shows me he was always in trouble," I said to Colleen.

"He was," she said. "He was in rehab a couple of times, but he was always in trouble. He was kicked out of school for bringing a knife."

"When he died, he shows me someone looked at him and said, 'What a waste,'" I continued.

"I think a lot of people said that," she answered.

"He tells me, 'Every moment that is passed breathing in and breathing out is a moment of equal value, one moment to the next.' Whether you are productive, or serving people, or bettering yourself, or not – your life is as valuable from one moment to the next."

"That doesn't sound like him," Colleen said.

"Maybe not when he was alive in the physical world," I replied. "But remember that where he is now he has complete understanding. He says, 'Stop the judgment.' You don't have to do something to be beloved. You don't have to do something to be perfect, you just have to be. Just drawing breath, just being alive in the world from one moment to the next is of extraordinary value. A value of one hundred, as high as you can go. Whether you're drawing breath in the service of somebody else or you're drawing breath doodling and daydreaming, the very miracle of being alive is not directly proportional to whether or not you're doing something. Just being here. Nothing is wasted, no time has been lost. There's nothing to catch up to. He tells me, 'When we think about people who've passed or we think about ourselves this way, every single moment is valuable; every single moment is of equal value to the next.'"

Colleen had a hard time believing that wisdom such as this could come from a kid who didn't have enough smarts to keep himself out of detention. Yet so impassioned was his message, that I studied it for a long time after our reading was over. Very often it's those people who were the worst abusers or made the stupidest mistakes who come through from the spirit world with such profound messages. Who better to understand the beauty of love and peace than those who felt so far away from it when alive?

Meditation for Understanding Your Inherent Spiritual Health
(10:19)

Remember, find the way the message works for you. If you are a visual person, picture the suggestions in your mind's eye. If you connect more to sound, imagine sound or vibration moving through you. If you're a feeling person, let yourself imagine that you actually can feel what the meditation suggests. Feel free to adjust any of the wording to suit you. This meditation takes approximately ten minutes, but can be shortened by skipping the relaxation at the beginning. Remember the keys to successful self-suggestion:

Every time you pay attention to an idea on purpose, with intention, it gets easier the next time. Repeat, repeat, repeat!

Use different images every time if you feel like it. There's no need to rigidly adhere to the same suggestions.

If something in this meditation doesn't quite resonate with you, tweak it. You must speak to your own subconscious mind in language or with examples you find acceptable.

If you're creating your own script, be sure to keep your suggestions in the present tense and define the positive outcome. For example, say "My spirit is whole and complete," rather than "I'm not broken."

If you'd like to, record yourself reading this script. Be sure to make any adjustments you think will be beneficial for your unique situation. Otherwise, have a general understanding of the path this script takes and recreate it in your mind. The words are not magic; if you don't recall it exactly during your meditation, that's okay. If you prefer to listen to a free recorded version of this script, go to: *http://liveandlearnguides.com/specialbookoffer/*

Some days you'll meditate easily and feel terrific. Other days you may only be able to settle in for a few minutes. That's okay. Repetition is more important than depth of trance.

Plan a time to do this. When we tell ourselves we're going to do something, we are more likely to follow through. Inform yourself that you will do this nightly as you're falling asleep, or sitting in the car for a few minutes before heading home from work.

If you're listening to the free recorded version you'll hear a tone before the relaxation countdown (*************) and again at the end. To skip the relaxation countdown, fast forward to the second tone and begin listening then.

Sit up or lie back comfortably. Close your eyes, and breathe naturally and normally.

You are now using your mind on purpose, to build your confidence in yourself and in your dreams. You'll soon recognize or remember that you are an immortal, perfect soul. There is a part of you that is untouched by rejection, fear, or grief. This part of you is ever bright, shining, whole, and perfect. Let's go there now.

(Skip the section between the asterisks if your time is limited or you tend to fall asleep easily)

****

In a moment you'll be imagining a profound inward journey. As you count from ten down to one, picture or think of yourself spiralling comfortably into the deepest, safest, holiest part of your mind.

10: There is an inner space within you. Decide now that you'll be adventurous and explore. You're going on a journey to the center of your Self. Your body will become increasingly relaxed as you go.

9: There may be some heat or resistance as you break through the atmosphere. Go anyway. You'll be amazed if you allow yourself to fly there. You may notice that all muscles in your face, jaw, throat, and neck are beginning to relax.

8: Feel your back against the chair or bed, feel it relax as all tension drains away. Your thinking mind is relaxing as you go deeper into the imaginative mind.

7: You may brush up against resistance as you travel in. Memories, perceptions, doubting voices. Let yourself fall weightless towards this extraordinary place in the center of You. Let that resistance fly right by you like space debris.

6: The front of your body relaxes, you breathe comfortably. Imagine as you drift inward that now you can see, like a pinprick in the distance, a dot of bright, welcoming light.

5: As your legs relax, and your feet and toes, imagine you are really enjoying the weightlessness of space. What a comfortable, delightful feeling! Breathing naturally and normally, notice that the pinprick of light has grown bigger as you get closer.

4: You're being drawn towards this bright clear light, closer and closer. It's like a glorious sun, welcoming, protective, safe, and comfortable. A deep sense of peace comes over you as you allow yourself to be drawn effortlessly towards this amazing energy.

3: The light is all around you now, and it feel so wonderful to have it wash over you. All fatigue, worry, stress, and sadness falls away. A sense of excitement seems to build, as if you were returning to a place where you felt the best. A place where you felt welcome, free, and happy.

2: Feeling lighter and lighter, drifting into the center of this serene yet energetic place. Totally relaxed.

1: Let yourself slow to a stop right in the center of this light, floating weightlessly within it. You are in the light, and the light is in you.

****

Imagine yourself now, right in the middle of a perfect sun. This light is cleansing, purifying, and protecting you. You are totally safe. It can be any color you like; the colors may even change as you explore here. That's perfectly normal.

As you consider this light, you begin to see that, in many ways, it defines you. In the light you cannot see your body, your clothing, or your hair. You can only see light, and that feels so true and comfortable. This light overpowers and outshines your physical presence in every way.

Within the light you feel great joy and steadiness. You cannot see pain, hurt, or sorrow. You see only light, around and within you. There's no interruption; there's nothing that can dim this light.

Within this light you feel power and connection. You understand that you are limitless and eternal. There is no age here, just being. No physical reflection here, just light. With great relief and acceptance, you understand that this is you!

You are this light, this perfect, shining, irreducible, beacon of life. You have always been, and you will always be. There is nothing in this light that needs correction or fixing. Everything is as it should be, just as you are now.

Take a moment to look around you: notice that off in the distance, floating in this weightlessness are other lights just as brilliant and perfect as yours. As you understand that these lights are others in your world, you begin to see their perfection, too. These are your loved ones, your friends, your beloved pets, your children. Every one a perfect, shining light. Faultless and serene.

Look a little closer and see that between all of these brilliant, glorious suns there are webs of light connecting you to each other. You may begin to feel that your heart is filling up with love and compassion for the uniqueness and perfection of all these spheres of life.

Imagine looking up now, in your mind's eye, right from the center of your own holy light. Perhaps you can see above you the most brilliant light of all, the One from which all of these other suns were created. How beautiful! How perfect! The rays of that profound light come right to you and to all the others. The connection is unmistakable. You realize that the source of your light is flooding you with love and bottomless energy. A beautiful, unspeakable vibration of well-being washes over you as you realize that your spirit, your light is a perfect creation, a perfect copy, connected to every other spirit.

Take as long as you like to enjoy this feeling, this understanding of your true nature and your true relationships.

****

Pause here to take as much time as you need. If you're listening to the pre-recorded version, you can pause that recording now for as long as you like.

****

When you're ready, tell yourself you can return here anytime. In the meantime in your daily life you will always remember that you are not your body, your bank account, or your habits. You are not defined by the ego that is a natural part of every human being. There is no part of your spirit that is broken, wrong, or faulty. You are eternal, perfect, and whole. The light at the center of your spirit can power great change in your self-reflection, your actions, habits, and body – if you so desire. From now on, you learn from your mistakes, you treat yourself and others with great compassion and tolerance. You recognize on all the levels of your mind that you and all people have a healthy, whole, perfect spirit, and you naturally become more forgiving of yourself and others, more tolerant, more easy going.

You know deep in your spirit that you cannot be dimmed. The mind may try to convince you it's possible that parts of you are broken, but deep inside you know the truth. You are a good person. A brilliant life. The world needs you. Your light is very important. Your voice is valuable, necessary, and a key part of the perfection of all humankind. You allow yourself the confidence to believe these ideas, and to allow your inner spirit to drive you towards improvements in behavior or actions, if you so desire.

Your confidence in your ultimate well-being grows with every second of every minute of every hour of every day. And there is nothing – no thought, feeling, memory, sensation, idea, or person from the past, the present, or ever to come in the future – which can convince you that your light is anything but perfect.

Take a deep breath now, and exhale. One more, and breathe out gently. When you're ready, open your eyes and let yourself carry these wonderful feelings of light on to the next task you have to do, and throughout the rest of the day.

PART TWO

*"The voyage to discovery is not in seeking new landscapes,
but in having new eyes."*
Marcel Proust

The Spirit Condition

In this section of the book our loved ones share their views on being spirit people, on God, Heaven, past lives, and communicating with us. This information was gathered from many different spirit people over many circles and readings. I cannot claim with absolute certainty that these stories exactly represent the afterlife. The spirits don't show me temples and throne rooms, but they do show me love and acceptance.

With the exception of a few topics, the spirit people aren't too forthcoming on the afterlife itself. I'm not sure if this is because their experience in the spirit world is beyond our ability to comprehend, if adequate words to describe it just don't exist, or if it's because Heaven is different for every spirit person.

My clients often ask me if their loved ones are together, and even this is a difficult question to answer with certainty. It's clear that loved ones in spirit come in together during a reading, but are they together in a geographical sense? I just don't know. Some spirit people, especially husband and wife couples, will indicate they are together. A deceased child will often appear in the company of a loved one who was older at the time of passing, such as a grandparent. Those associations are comforting to my clients, but I wonder if the spirit people are presenting these pictures as evidence of their identity rather than as evidence of their afterlife experience.

For example, I recently had a lovely grandmother come in during a message circle. Her granddaughter was able to identify her immediately through specific characteristics I offered. Shortly after, the husband – my client's grandfather – came through. The spirit couple indicated they were deeply in love and had been throughout their lives. This was a key piece of identity evidence for my client, as her whole family admired the grandparents' love story. My client was happy to know that her beloved grandparents were together, as she expected they would be. Were they occupying the same space in Heaven, or did they come in showing their togetherness because it was such a strong identifier for them? I don't know for certain.

It comforts us to know that loved ones are cared for by those who have gone before, and on a number of occasions I've shared messages from spirit people who were met by other previously deceased family members. Spirit people also speak about being met by dogs, cats, horses, even pet birds, when they've gone out to the afterlife.

Part of me feels assured that our loved ones exist together in their spirit form, although my rational mind would prefer a little more proof. I've been told that time and space don't exist in the spirit world the way they do here in our physical world, and that may be why we can't have a rational understanding of the structure of the afterlife. I've read descriptions by psychics and mediums who have a clear idea what Heaven looks like, defining physical places like temples, libraries, and throne rooms. But we all have a different concept about what riches mean, or how libraries and temples feel, so I'm unconvinced that we would all be received into such places and understand them equally as "Heaven." For me, a Heavenly place would be the bright, frigid side of a steep mountain, with challenging work ahead of me and a breathtaking view all around. As a former high altitude mountaineer, this environment feels closer to God than any temple I've ever been in. But I can see how for many people a dangerous ridge on a remote mountain in the Andes would not feel Heavenly at all!

What I have heard repeatedly from spirit people is what *they* are like in the afterlife. Time and again our loved ones report being their best selves in the spirit world. They'll present a physical self that reflects their finest hour: athletic young people will show physical strength; beautiful women appear at their loveliest once again; a soldier who lost a limb in combat will present himself as whole. They also talk about their emotional selves: now in the afterlife they are free of fear, prejudice, anger, guilt, judgment, and sin. Hard as it is to believe, I have yet to meet a spirit person who maintains a grudge after death. Though I've never met them in life or in spirit, I suspect even the Hatfields and McCoys now get along just fine in the afterlife.

I was presenting at a women's club in Westchester County, New York one freezing winter night. As part of the evening's entertainment I was talking to the group about mediumship, telling some funny stories and sprinkling in a few readings as spirit people came in. I love to do these kinds of events as it gives me a wonderful opportunity to make a connection and then explain how it feels, how it came about, and how a person might practice such a thing on her own.

During this talk, I brought through a man who was showing me a particular type of ring. It was big, bulky, and expensive, neither a school ring nor a wedding ring. He showed me diabetes, a connection to trains, and a mild speech impediment towards the end of his life. A woman in the audience knew immediately who he was. This spirit kept flashing the ring in front of her and smiling, so I asked the significance. The woman said her father had earned a diamond for each year he sold a certain number of cars, and he was a superior salesman.

"Well, he's showing this ring and laughing about it," I said.

"He's probably still mad about it," she answered.

"No," I said, "he's laughing. Spirit people don't stay mad."

"Oh, he would still be mad!" she retorted.

"No," I said again. "He is showing me that he is laughing. He is not mad for any reason about this ring."

"Yes, he would be," she insisted one last time, and I let it drop there. She came up to me at the end of the night and told me her uncle had stolen the ring, and her father had been truly upset about it. Despite my assurances, she couldn't accept that her dad was no longer fuming about his brother and the theft of this prized possession. Perhaps my guest wasn't prepared to forgive the still-living uncle who'd upset her father for so long. Maybe she felt it would be disloyal to his memory to believe that all was forgiven.

The spirit people want us to know that they take only the best part of their character into the afterlife – their love, understanding, compassion, and tolerance – even if they had it only in a microscopic degree when they were alive in the physical world.

You Might Want To Know...

What We're Like

Spirit people report that they remain here with us and possess everything we loved about them, but in a different form. I know this is small comfort when we long to put our arms around him or hear her voice, but we are encouraged to focus on what it is about the *spirit* of a person we love. We are connecting with so much more than the physical. If we weren't, an old man wouldn't look longingly at his now-elderly wife and still see the beautiful girl he married. Parents wouldn't look at their adult children and still see the joyful kids playing in the house. Our energies are the connection. We're connected by what we love about each other and the light we see in the eyes of a loved one. This is why we feel the same whether we're seventeen or seventy: what makes us *us* is immortal.

One spirit man came through for his son, my client, who was struggling with his loss. The father in spirit assured him that he remained present in his son's life.

"We're like water: two hydrogen molecules and one oxygen molecule," I said. "He tells me, 'Whether a vapor or frozen solid, the elemental structure is identical. Water is made up of H_2O, though our experience of it changes when it's below 32°F or above 212°F. I'm like the vapor now. I used to be solid, as you are, but now I'm like steam. I'm the same, though your experience of me feels less solid.'"

Spirit people seem to exist in a state of energy, so they may show me just one significant body part to identify themselves. One man in spirit showed me his huge nose. His entire family recognized him immediately. He took our brief connection to power through a single identifying factor. It was much easier for me to describe that one part than to describe every wrinkle, expression, or posture had I seen the entire man. Recently a grandmother showed me just her glass eye, to the delight of her family. No other physical description was required. I've seen amputated limbs, tattoos, and deformities. One young husband came through with an enormous erection, which his wife found particularly endearing (though I was blushing madly).

I usually see distinguishing characteristics rather than the whole person. For example, in a recent reading I had the feeling of an older man with congestive heart failure who showed me a full head of white hair. When I offered this to my client (who had already identified her grandfather), she said, "What else do you see?"

Instead I described how I felt – which is the other way spirit people give me impressions.

"I feel as though it's difficult to walk, my feet are painful, as though my skin is stretched tight over my ankles and feet," I said. "My feet and ankles are swollen and I can't walk on them except to shuffle just a few steps."

"But what does he look like?" she asked me again.

"I don't know," I said. "I'm shown a full head of white hair and these swollen feet. Can you acknowledge these two things?"

"Yes," she said, "his feet were always propped up and he couldn't wear shoes anymore because his feet were so swollen."

"What about his hair?" I asked.

"Totally snow white," was her reply. "He was so proud of it. What does the rest of him look like?" she asked.

"I don't know," I said again. "He shows me things about himself that you can identify, and that's what I'm getting. Spirit people don't have unlimited energy to communicate through me, so they're going to give me a couple of specific things that are unique to them."

"But if you can't see him, maybe he's not there!" she cried.

Suddenly, I understood what she was asking. My client's concern, because I couldn't describe him from head to toe in a visual sense, was that her grandfather wasn't there or wasn't whole. Once I explained that I see spirit people in flashes and parts, not as though I'm looking at a three-dimensional body, she was satisfied that her loved one was okay.

I don't know if all mediums see spirit people the way I do, so I can only report my personal experience. Maybe spirits do live in three-dimensional bodies somewhere in the afterlife; I simply don't know and I can't imagine that anyone on this side of the veil can comment on this with certainty.

What I have seen and feel personally sure of, is that the essence of our loved ones persists into the afterlife. As the spirit father mentioned in the first part of this section, *who* the spirit people are is still fundamentally the same, though *what* they are may have changed form.

How We See You

Spirit people have a lot to say about who we are as physical beings. I hear from them often that we don't value ourselves enough. In the afterlife, they can see our tremendous worth, our capacity for love, forgiveness, and tolerance, and they often seem astonished that we don't always see it ourselves.

My client Lena is not native to the United States, though she lives here now with her husband. During one of our readings her grandmother came through, first to encourage Lena's plans to travel to her home country and visit the family living there. Lena hadn't told anyone her plans, though she'd been researching flight prices just that afternoon. Once the connection with her grandmother in spirit was firmly established, the spirit lady got right to the point using a symbol I'd seen many times before.

"She shows me the lens in a lighthouse," I said, "and wants me to make a comparison for you. In this image the light itself is small, but the lens around it enhances the light exponentially. Because of the lens, the light can be seen through the fog, for miles and miles, despite distance and time." I paused for a moment, as the second part of the message became clear.

"Don't worry if your own light seems small. You have around you this enormous reflecting lens requiring no effort of your own. We're with you regardless of distance or time." The spirit grandmother went on to chastise Lena lovingly for her overly-humble nature. My client couldn't see that the very fact she was alive made a difference in the world, because she couldn't see the breadth of the world's reaction to her. From the spirit world, Lena's grandmother could see how far Lena's love, compassion, good humor, and forgiveness was rippling out, and wanted to assure her that her actions made a difference, across all time and space.

About Guidance

I'm often asked if our loved ones in the spirit world act as guardian angels. Spirits do intervene by causing us to delay, causing us to notice something just at the right time, even by pulling or pushing us out of the way of danger in a few extreme examples. More commonly, our loved ones who have passed away try to guide us in our self perception. Having gone out to the spirit world, they understand what comes with us and what stays behind, how beloved and forgiven we are, and how we might enjoy our lives here in the physical world if we could only cease judging.

Shara came in for an individual reading and was met by a friend in spirit who gave her advice about spiritual and human guidance.

"Your friend says, 'Allow people to help you.' People can guide you, but be aware that they may be able to show you just one possibility," I said. "You don't have to figure it all out yourself."

"I let people guide me," my client replied rather morosely.

"She wants you to know people can guide you with their ideas. You might not even have known such ideas were possibilities. Keep your ears and eyes open. Signs are everywhere. Guides are everywhere."

"Where?" Shara asked.

"She says, 'Every person is a guide.' You can seek guidance, but it also comes through on its own. The supernatural guidance that you weren't looking for. She's referring to people who may be able to guide you without being aware that this is what they're doing. Many more options for guidance exist than you can imagine for yourself."

This friend in spirit recognized (though I didn't at the time) that Shara was feeling untethered and alone before some rather important decisions. Through insecurity and overanalysis, Shara had artificially reduced her scope of possibilities. Her loved one in spirit reminded her that *the spirit* of any person, living or dead, may represent signs or guidance if we are willing to see that way.

Shara's maternal grandfather also came in during this reading with a similar message of guidance. After identifying him through the evidence he impressed on me, the spirit grandfather gave this message:

"He tells me that he's still listening to you. Or he's still listening. He's still participating in the family and likes to be spoken to or asked for advice."

"How can I do that?" Shara asked.

"He says, 'We're still alive, even though we're not in the physical form.' He says, 'Go ahead and ask me,' because he can bring some influence to bear on your personal clarity. He can't move mountains, maybe, but he can direct your attention in a certain way. He can shift energies in a certain direction."

***

Another client of mine announced right at the beginning of our session that she was skeptical. I always like having clients such as this because I enjoy watching the skepticism fall away as their loved ones in the spirit world offer undeniable evidence of their presence at our reading. I respect skepticism as long as it comes with an open mind. Nelissa was just such a client. Her mother in spirit came through, whom Nelissa most wanted to contact. Her sudden passing had left my client and her sisters feeling at loose ends. Our session was nearly over, after many happy tears and much relief, when Nelissa asked me, "Is she around us all the time? My sisters and I?"

"Is she around you all the time," I repeated, knowing consciously that Nelissa wanted to hear a solid affirmation.

"The answer is, 'It depends,'" I said. "This is the symbol she's giving me. She shows me those thermometers that have the floating disks in them. Do you know what kind I mean? It's a clear tube with some sort of oil in it, with different beads that float up and down to indicate the temperature."

"I know what you mean," Nelissa replied.

"Whether she can come down and be with you is dependent on her energy level," I said. "This is not entirely under her control. It may be because she is new to the spirit world, or maybe she doesn't know how to do it yet. She says, 'For all the significant moments I will be there.' She's talking about inspiration, and that one of the things she'll be able to do best is inspire." Nelissa's mother in spirit went on to mention being present when a baby was born in the family and at other important events in the lives of her children.

How We Stay Connected

My grandmother passed away in her mid-nineties after a lifetime of love, industry, and devotion to God. *Babcie*, as we called her, which is Polish for grandmother, had her wits about her until near the very end, and we were so grateful to have had her in our lives. Of course, I was saddened by her passing, but I knew she was rejoining my grandfather and that she was more than ready to go home to the spirit world. A few days before her funeral my mother asked me to speak about my grandmother at the reception. I wanted to define my grandmother's immortal spirit as succinctly as I could, and I decided to go right to the source. In a meditation (which can be found at the end of this section), I reached out to my Babcie and asked her for inspiration.

Once in the meditative trance, my Babcie took me on a tour of her house as it looked when I was a girl. Everywhere I looked in the house I saw her artwork. There was the still life painting in the kitchen; upstairs was another of a doe in the woods. In the front bedroom was the mysterious and fascinating portrait of a girl; her rendering of their rustic summer camp hung above the desk upstairs.

I looked at those paintings as I did once before as a girl, wishing and hoping that I could be an artist. When I was young I watched my mother sketch and paint, and I prayed some artistic ability would come to me, too. In this visit with my Babcie in spirit, she showed me the ribbon that connected us: a ribbon of art emanating from my grandmother, down through my mother, and right into me. When she showed me this I was acutely aware of that forgotten little-girl wish, especially as she reminded me that I'd had an entire career as a successful graphic designer.

The ribbon that connected us came down through time and space. I know we were connected through the family and through our DNA, but this ribbon of connection was somehow additionally special. Even though she's gone into the spirit world, this connection is still vibrant and alive. My Babcie is still vibrant and alive, in me and in the artwork I've done and will continue to do. I will never forget her, what she gave to me, or how the ribbon of art connects us through my mother. As my meditation concluded, my grandmother drew us both back for a greater perspective on connections. She showed me that along with the ribbon of artistic talent that connected us, she had many other ribbons connecting her to others: the troupe she danced with, the other volunteers at the hospital where she worked, the lives she touched at her job and in her neighborhood. So many connections! Ribbons of talent, memories, DNA – Babcie showed me so beautifully how we impact each other continually, regardless of time and space. If I could have painted a picture at that moment in my meditation, my beloved grandmother would look like a May Pole, with bright ribbons going out in all directions to each life she touched and to all the generations that will follow, until the end of time.

Since that day, many spirit people have used the ribbon symbol to indicate to my clients how they are still connected, and what our loved ones in the spirit world mean when they say, "We are alive in you."

***

My client Carol had been to see me with a group, and came back later for a one-on-one reading. After connecting her with several loved ones who had passed away, I felt the incoming presence of a spirit person new to the assembled group.

"A woman comes in giving me a feeling of great irritation in my throat, which usually indicates a smoker, " I said. "She gives me this feeling of having medical intervention in her throat. She passed around retirement age – not old, but past her working years. She is a little bit concerned about keeping up her appearance. She shows me coloring her hair well past the point when it was gray, and wearing make-up."

"That's my grandmother," said Carol. "She was a heavy smoker and had emphysema. She had a tube to help her breathe before she died."

"People took a lot from her," I continued. "She gave to the point of being drained. She shows this around you, too. You may be pouring out your energy. Look at your relationships and make sure they're not draining you dry."

"Wow, that is totally on target!" said Carol. "We definitely have that in common."

"There's more," I said. "Did she fry something in particular, because she shows me a frying pan. I see a particular food she prepared in a frying pan."

"Yes," replied Carole

"She shows me you also make this," I said.

"Yes, I do," she answered.

"Your grandmother is showing me this connection, this passing-down. There's much warmth and affection from her to you because you do what she did. This connection looks like a ribbon, and she says, 'I'm alive in you because you do this.'"

Carol's grandmother showed her two ways in which they were still connected, one of which she advised against, and the other that the spirit woman enjoyed participating in.

***

In a different reading, a grandfather came in to point out the timeless value of our interwoven lives.

"Here is a man who passed in his seventies," I said to my client, Mark. "He is robust, several extra pounds all over, somewhat barrel-chested. Not obese, but solidly built. He wears glasses with thick plastic frames. A little bit of thinning hair, not bald,. More salt than pepper. He appears as a patriarch, someone around whose table everyone sat. Not a particularly gregarious guy. People didn't sit around because they loved to listen to his stories, but because he was the patriarch. I have an old-world feeling," I finished. "He's first generation in this country."

"Definitely my grandfather," said Mark. "You described him perfectly. I was a little scared of him because he wasn't friendly to us kids, but everyone kowtowed to him."

"Just as people may have sat around his table, he shows me people are all around his bed in the hospital. Everyone is with him," I said. "When he was going to be removed from life support all the family gathered around. He witnessed everyone take a turn saying goodbye to him one at a time."

"That's right," Mark replied. "He was taken off a ventilator. Right before that we each said an indiviual goodbye."

"I see a tradition... what is this?" I interrupted myself. Sometimes a spirit will give me a feeling to translate, and if I'm translating incorrectly the spirit interrupts me with a new symbol or a better way to say what he means.

"He has this message: there are traditional values. No, that's not what I mean either!" I laughed. "Let me try again. He says family traditions and those things that we keep alive from our collective past truly give a sense of continuity. That allows new people to come in and be braided together as part of the collective or tradition, and when people pass away we can let them go and know that we're all part of a line. He shows me a rope or a braid being woven together through time and new people will come in and be added to the family. All the way back in time it's become this strong, powerful line that's made up of all those who came before. If one of the little threads in the rope snaps, it's still woven in all the way into the past and hasn't diminished the strength of the rope at all."

I could see the image of this woven rope perfectly, but wasn't sure I had conveyed the grandfather's symbolism correctly. I asked him for another way to say his message.

"He says, 'We can let go of who we need to say goodbye to when they pass away, and we can welcome whoever comes in, if we remember where we come from and keep alive some family traditions.' If you have a family tradition you create a sense of continuity, of being woven into a strong fabric. It influences people down the line, also. This helped his family let go of him, and the traditions that he had still keep the family together. Traditions are important to people who are passing away and to people who are joining in, and to the whole braid of your family, together."

Mark replied that the message made complete sense to him and that his family was talking about traditions and his grandfather just the weekend before. Like the ribbon my own grandmother showed me from the spirit world, this gentleman indicated our continuity in depth of time and breadth of our present day relationships.

The Timelessness of Life

Lori's good friend who passed from ovarian cancer came through in a private reading.

"She shows me a tapestry," I said, "and she says, 'I wove this tapestry with my life, and now I get to look at it.' She means she gets to look at in the spirit world."

"That's a lovely thought," said Lori.

"Every day in her physical life she added to this tapestry and when she went into the spirit world she could reflect on it, and this brings her a great deal of enjoyment. It's similar to looking at a child's drawing, where we might say, 'Oh isn't that beautiful.'"

"Actually she was an artist so it makes sense that she'd show that picture to you," replied Lori.

"She says, 'It's not as sophisticated as where we are now, but I can still appreciate the beauty and creativity in it.' She wove it with her spirituality and just by her daily existence, and now where she is in the spirit world she looks at it and is moved with compassion for herself. She shows me she's touched by her efforts and her spiritual seeking, and she has an enormous amount of love – this is interesting – an enormous amount of love for *herself* when she was here."

Never having seen anything like this from a spirit person before, Lori and I continued to talk about this extraordinary image. Her friend showed us her life, her challenges, her spiritual seeking, her efforts, even her failures, as all part of a picture she was weaving, simply because she was alive in the physical world. After passing she got to enjoy the picture she didn't even know she was creating. We were astonished by her description of how by looking at her work she could see her whole life, not for the purpose of reviewing good deeds and bad, but to see the beauty of her own existence as a spirit operating in a human world with ego, personality, and disease. Like looking at a child's best effort, she was moved by compassion and love for the person she was when she was alive. Both Lori and I felt encouraged by her friend's message. Knowing we sometimes made colossal errors in judgment in the past, we both felt hopeful that we, too, might regard some of our own experiences as that of a child trying her best.

Her friend in spirit shared not one iota of self-judgment when looking at her creation, and this was the most uplifting news of all. Many mediums and other so-called spiritual persons report that, after passing, we review our earthly life with a judgmental eye, sometimes in the company of spirit guides. In all the years I've been talking to spirit people in the afterlife, none has undergone such a procedure upon death.

***

I tried to share this good news with a client recently, during a reading in which his father came through in spirit. My client Craig told me he was no longer a practicing Christian, and he didn't believe God would forgive his sins.

"Which sins are you talking about?" I asked him. I'm not qualified to take confession, but I hoped I might help Craig see his "sins" differently.

"I never believed women could love me, so I never loved them," he answered. "I just had sexual relationships."

"And you think that's a sin?" I asked.

"Well, I didn't think I could be loved," he said. "One of my girlfriends had an abortion. I don't think God will forgive me for that."

"Why not?" I asked.

"Because we killed that baby," he answered.

"Your father shows me something and he's not laughing now," I said. His father had been jumping in during our reading with his natural joking manner. "He tells me that a person cannot kill anything. He says, 'We don't create life, and we can't end it.' He shows me that an immortal spirit comes into a human body to live out a human life. The humans make the body and humans may destroy the body, but that's completely separate from the immortal spirit life, the way he's showing it."

"That doesn't make any sense!" said Craig.

"It would if you could see the picture in my mind!" I laughed. "Let me try this again. Your father shows me that life, the energy that makes you *you*, has always been around. It wasn't created and it can't be destroyed. It had no beginning, and it won't disappear when you die – just as your father's spirit has not disappeared just because his human body stopped functioning."

"Because energy cannot be created or destroyed, only transformed," said Craig, a retired chemistry teacher.

"Exactly!" I said. "So sure, someone might murder someone else, or alternatively save someone's life, but your father shows me that it's important to distinguish Life-with-a-capital-L from human life. Those two kinds of life come together for a short period of time, and human life obviously begins and ends, but the spirit that sparks that human life is timeless and immortal."

People feel strongly about abortion, miscarriage, and contraception, and it's neither my desire nor my place to preach on the subject of whether or not life begins at conception. Everyone should feel comfortable enough with his own values that he can live by them without needing to convert anyone else to his way of thinking. In my practice as a medium, I have seen aborted fetuses, unbaptized babies, killers, suicides, and criminals all welcomed in the spirit world. I try to remember that *who* we are is immortal, and as humans we can learn from any mistakes we make so that our lives can be better.

***

Barbara's mother in spirit came through during a message circle, and Barb readily identified her. Barb's sweetheart Tom was with us in the circle, too, though he wished only to observe and not be read himself.

"Your mother wants to answer Tom's question," I said, surprising myself. "She shows me, Tom, that you have a question about the afterlife. About life after death, in general."

"I'm not sure how it's possible," he said, shrugging. "I want to believe, but I don't see how, if a person dies – you see them die and you know they're not in that body anymore.... Where does the person go?"

"Good question! Let's ask her," I said. "She's showing me Aquarius the water bearer. She says to you, 'Life isn't a water jug which pours out its contents and stops when the jug is empty. It's continually pouring out. The jar is never empty; life doesn't come out over the period of time it takes to empty the jug and then - oops, nothing left in there, goodbye. Life is continually pouring out.'"

All of these images: the ribbon, the braid, the woven image, the immortal spirit life, the endless flowing water, all beautifully express how our spirits are timeless and eternal despite the creation and the inevitable destruction of the human body.

***

In two recent readings the spirit people showed me another interpretation of the timelessness of life. First, a mother who'd committed suicide came through for my client Nicky. The family remained baffled over their mother's choice to take her life, and Nicky hoped to connect with her mother for some answers.

"She holds her arms in a V for victory," I said, after Nicky's mother had given several pieces of evidence identifying her spirit. "When she made this final decision, she wasn't afraid. She didn't go shaking into this act. She tells me that this is important information for you today."

"None of us could believe she did it," answered Nicky. "She had a chronic illness, but it wasn't terminal. I just keep thinking she must have been so afraid." Nicky began to cry as she tormented herself with what she imagined were her mother's last moments.

"Wait a minute," I said. "Listen to your mother. She felt this was her only option, so when she made her decision she felt something like relief. I'm not going to say happiness, but relief. After the decision had been made, it was almost an easy thing to do. She wasn't afraid, that's why she gives me this sense of victory. She passed through that experience and on the other side of it realized, 'I've taken all that is wonderful and whole and perfect about me and I left behind what was troubled and sore.' She is victorious over death and not a victim of death."

***

This was the first time I'd seen a spirit person show victory over death. The second time came in a reading not long after Nicky's. Jean was part of a larger message circle when her friend Pamela came through in spirit. Pamela showed two battles against cancer, succumbing quickly the second time, which Jean acknowledged.

"She points to her mid-section, and I feel she is talking about ovarian cancer," I said to Jean.

"She did have that, but it's not what she died from," said Jean.

"Pamela indicates ovarian cancer, and taking a traditional medical route to healing," I answered. "Chemo, radiation, losing her hair, all of that process."

"Yes, that's right," Jean answered.

"She shows me more than a year, almost two years, and then feeling a lump. You told her to jump right on that, get right back to the doctor," I said, looking at Jean.

"I did, I just had a feeling it wasn't good," she said.

"And you were right," I replied.

"Now she shows me cancer again, but this time it's all over, in every part of her body. She declined the chemo and radiation route," I said.

"That's right," said Jean. "She wanted to try more natural things. Doctors told her she wasn't going to survive anyway, and she didn't want to be ill in her last months. She wanted to be able to enjoy time with her family."

"Everyone is gathered around her in her hospice bed," I said, as Jean nodded. "After she passes, everyone thinks, 'Oh, poor Pamela, she lost her battle to cancer.' Let me tell you, she is standing in front of you with her arms over her head, making a V for victory. She wants people to stop saying she lost her battle to cancer. She didn't lose, she is victorious."

Jean didn't say anything, though she looked at me as though I was crazy.

"This is the message: Pamela equates being alive to driving a car, and dying to a wall we run into at the end of our course. Because hitting that wall stops all forward motion, we conclude that living must stop also. We all have this perception, and Pamela did, too. It seemed to her and to her family that she was speeding towards a solid, impenetrable wall. That's life. It goes along until it hits a wall, then it's over.

"But here's the interesting part. She shows me speeding towards this solid wall that is our expectation of what death will be like... and the second, the instant she's upon the wall, it completely disappears and she continues to speed forward. She never hit anything! Nothing came to a stop! It's amazing, this feeling she gives me. She didn't die!

Not in the way that we think. Her life didn't hit a wall and stop, it streaked right up to that wall where she and everyone watching braced for impact and... nothing. Peace. Life. Just moving forward, still."

"Wow, I don't know what to say!" said Jean.

"Neither do I!" I replied. "It's crucial that you know and that her family knows, she didn't die. Well, maybe you can't say it just like that. But she didn't experience death, not the way everyone feared and expected. She *triumphed* over death. *She* beat death. Death didn't beat her. This is why she doesn't want you to say she lost the battle to cancer. She *won* the battle, because she overcame the Great Obstacle. She disproved the great hypothesis. She is thoroughly triumphant."

God and The Heavenly Afterlife

Many years ago during an amazing energy healing treatment, I felt the message, "You are God's thought of Himself." Not just me, of course. I understood that message to mean that every spirit in a human body was a living reflection of God. I use the masculine pronoun because it's convenient and common, though I believe that God has neither masculine nor feminine traits as we know them. I believe God is both Mother and Father, a divine Parent, who created and values both men and women equally.

Some religions teach that God created human life so He could experience Himself. Others suggest we are extensions of God, or that we broke away from Him and are always trying to find our way back so we can become whole again. What these theories have in common is that we are all part of the Creator. More than one spirit person has referenced this reflective nature of humankind.

Two women in spirit came through for my guests Lauren and Marianne during a message circle. The guests were acquainted with each other though their two spirit grandmothers, who came in layered over one another, had never met. As they often do, spirit people will use a ribbon to show an extra connection with a guest; usually indicating a shared name or talent. A common bloodline or hereditary medical condition is usually symbolized with a DNA spiral.

Alberta came in first, the grandmother of Lauren. She showed me a ribbon to Lauren, though Lauren could not connect a name between the two of them. Alberta then introduced another spirit.

"Do you have an Ann or Anna in spirit?" I asked Lauren.

"I do," said Marianne, who was seated right next to her.

"Do you have Ann or Anna in your name, too?" I asked Marianne. She smiled for an answer until I recalled her name and started to laugh. "Oh, right, Mari-*anne.*"

"I'm going to stay with these two ladies, because they have something in common. Both are giving me the feeling of being alive in you. They taught you a skill or they have a name connection. They're alive in you, and are watching the extension of their lives play out in your lives. It gives them a warm feeling of satisfaction, as though they're still sharing in the wonderful challenge of physical life.

"Do you study mysticism?" I asked Marianne. She nodded in response.

"Marianne, your Anna wants to make an extra connection using a mystical example. She suggests that God created us to enjoy a reflection of Himself. He experiences Himself in His creations, and that gives Him great joy. Spirit people like Anna feel great joy, too, when they see a loved one who continues a talent or who shares a name; it's a reflection of their physical experience. That's what she means: Life is reflected back to her through you."

"That's pretty amazing," said Marianne.

"She's having so much fun knowing you're alive, being reflected in you. Following you through life gives her the feeling she is living again."

Alberta stepped forward again to indicate her other connection to Lauren. There wasn't a name in common, as we'd already determined, so I asked the spirit to be specific. She showed me a green thumb, so I mentioned Alberta's gardening skills.

"Oh my God, she could grow *anything!*" said Lauren. "I once saw her bring a dead Christmas cactus back to life. We joked she was like Jesus raising Lazarus from the dead!"

"Well, it's funny you should say that," I said to Lauren, "because you have this in common with her, and she's telling me it's like *you* raising *her* from the dead!"

Lauren looked a little nervous when I said that, so I continued, "I mean to say that Alberta is alive in you because you have the same skills and abilities with plants that she did."

"Well, I *am* pretty good with plants," Lauren agreed.

"Alberta is honoring the connection between the two of you that is separate from the genetic line, and saying that when you work lovingly and successfully with plants, in a way you are keeping her alive."

"Okay, I get it," she said.

"When your grandmother watches you express the same talent she had, she feels alive. She sees herself because you are a reflection of her. You're your own person, and in those moments when you're gardening, you're also part of your grandmother. That's what she feels, and sometimes you feel that, too," I said, listening with wonder to the words coming out of my mouth.

"Sometimes I do feel connected to her when I've got my hands in the dirt," Lauren said.

"She says, 'This is how God feels about us,'" I said, taking another long moment to let this sink in. The spirit people teach us so much in such simple ways. "She feels alive when you are a reflection of her, and says God feels this way when He sees us acting as a reflection of Him. He feels alive in us. We may even feel Him close by, just as you feel Alberta is with you when you're gardening."

I stopped the meter on our circle for a few minutes so all the guests could discuss this good news. It was astonishing to receive a spirit's perspective on how they see God participating in our lives. I understood that the more we act like or reflect God – compassionate, loving, tolerant, forgiving, and non-judgmental of ourselves and others – the more we feel connected to God, and feel His presence connected to us. Not for one moment did Alberta suggest that *not* acting like God meant He was distant from us. The spirit people enjoy watching and staying connected to us even if they see us making bad decisions, or if they were intolerable when alive in the human form. Their love and understanding for us is all they seem to carry into the spirit world. Alberta described God the same way: pure love and understanding. When we do what God does, He feels more alive in us.

Spirit people don't often talk about God as directly as Alberta did, but often use metaphors to get a divine message across. Maybe it's because true understanding of God is beyond us. Our loved ones in the afterlife use parables and symbols, just as Jesus did.

***

Renee's mother in spirit came through during a one-on-one reading. After Renee identified her, I went on with her message about going to a First Communion.

"Do you have an event like this planned? I think she's showing me this as a symbol, not a literal event." Whenever a spirit person shows me an image, ninety percent of the time it's intended to be symbolic. When I get an image in my mind's eye I usually wait to see what develops. If the image is followed by a feeling, memory, or idea, I know it's a metaphor for the message. If the image is static and persists just as it is, I know I should say exactly what I'm seeing. In this case, I had the feeling of a child's First Holy Communion, and spoke without waiting to see if more would develop. As the spirit people usually do, if I'm mistaken they'll correct me even if I'm in mid-sentence.

"It's probably a symbol," said Renee, "because I'm not aware of any First Communion."

"Your mother shows me a child's sacrament," I said. "If we can see through the eyes of a child, we have an opportunity to feel again that we are children in God."

"My mother was Catholic, and I've gone in another direction." Renee said.

"She's not telling you to go to church, but, 'to look at God the way you saw Him as a child.' For example, if I went to Disney World by myself, it wouldn't be so interesting, but if I took a child I'd get excited about it again. I would feel the newness through the child's eyes. You can reignite that sense of awe, the way a child might at a First Communion," I said, a little confused myself as I listened to my words.

"With God?" asked Renee.

"Yes, I mean the sense of awe about God," I answered.

"Is this a religious thing? Is she unhappy that I'm not practicing as a Catholic?" Renee asked

"No, no, this isn't about religion," I said, more sure now of what her mother in spirit was trying to get across to us. "She's indicating a way to feel awe about God again, and that doesn't mean you have to go to a Catholic church. There are many paths to God, and if you could see God again the way a child sees Him, you would feel the holiness of that."

"I'm not sure I get it, I don't see myself going back to being a Catholic," said Renee again.

"She's giving me a Catholic example because I was raised as a Catholic. She's using symbols I'm familiar with," I said. I explained to Renee that spirit people will use examples I have in my experience in order to get a message across. Renee's mother wanted to talk about connecting again with God by rediscovering the feeling of wonder a child has in celebrating Holy Communion for the first time.

"For a child there's a lot of wonder when she thinks about God. If the preparation and education is right, she understands that her First Communion will bring her closer to God. I see you were confirmed in the Catholic Church," I said.

"Yes," replied Renee, "though that was the last thing I ever did in church."

"She shows me St. Bernadette," I said. "Do you know this saint?"

"That was my confirmation name!" said Renee.

"I see a beam of light when you are at the altar. It's the sunlight, but it also feels more special than that."

"Oh my God, I was so freaked out!" Renee replied. "When it was my turn to go up to the altar, the sun came from behind a cloud and it got brighter in the church somehow. I was amazed! I thought God was watching me."

"That was a good feeling, though," I finished for her.

"Oh, yes," she said. "I didn't see the light come in for anyone in front of me, and it felt special. I don't know if it actually happened, it probably had nothing to do with God."

"*That's* what your mother is talking about!" I said. "That feeling of connection, of being singled out by God as a wonderful child. That's what she's talking about reigniting, *not* the grown-up part that says, 'Oh, I'm just making that up, I'm not special.'" I opened my eyes to see Renee had a big smile on her face.

"You know what I'm talking about now, right?" I asked her. "Your mother says, 'When we are awestruck again by the power of God, there's so much more that we can accomplish.' And this may be as basic as the power of positive thinking. When you feel special, you act a certain way. I'm not talking about arrogance, I mean the feeling of generosity you have when everything feels right. When life is good, a person is generous with praise, friendship, time, love, everything. Even with ourselves we're generous; we focus on our success. That's similar to a little child at First Communion or you at your Confirmation. Not the jaded adult who says that it's not real."

I loved this conversation with Renee, who began our reading with wry cynicism. She was on guard against what she initially perceived to be a message to go back to church, but her mother showed her a beautiful God-connection moment in her teenage years – a moment she hadn't told anyone about. Renee's defenses softened and her mother's message of love and empowerment found a place to land.

***

Natalia came to see me just a week after her sister Nola had been in for a private reading. Their mother had committed suicide, which I discovered when I brought the spirit through for Nola. When Natalia came in I reminded her that I'd already met her mother in spirit, so I would ask her to come through with different information about herself. Natalia informed me she'd listened to the recording I made at her sister Nola's reading, and even though she was astonished by information that I "couldn't have known," Natalia was still a bit skeptical. In addition to that, Natalia let me know she wasn't sure she believed in God or Heaven. When her mother in spirit came through with information I also could not have known, Natalia validated and engaged in the reading in a wonderful, active way. We had come to the end of our hour when I asked Natalia if she had any final questions.

"Does she think there's a God?" she asked.

"What a great question," I said, knowing that Natalia herself was deeply uncertain. At times like this, when I want to jump up and say "God is great! Please believe!" I must actively disengage my own judgment, opinion, beliefs, and rational mind. It's not always easy to separate my own feelings and beliefs from what the spirit people are giving me. It is my constant work to get myself out of the way and remove my ego entirely from the exchange.

"Here's the picture she shows me," I said. "Frequently, when we ask the spirit people about God or Heaven, they give us what we want to hear. Or, because they can't explain it very well, they'll give us a story that we could understand. But what she's showing me is that we *all* make up who God is. All of the spirits in the spirit world make up who God is. She doesn't want to say the word 'God,' though.

"Every time a spirit...," I stopped and started. This was getting difficult to translate. "A spirit doesn't leave this Collective [when she is born into human life] – but every time a spirit extends herself into the world, she is the whole Collective Spirit's expression of Itself. She's saying, 'We're all at the same time God and a reflection of God. She hesitates to say the word 'God,'" I repeated, "and I don't know if that's because she didn't believe or because of your atheistic leanings. Maybe she doesn't want to interfere with the process of your understanding of things. She's showing me what looks like a sun, which we are all part of. We all create this sense of completeness and wholeness.

"I think I get it," said Natalia.

"It's more of a Collective, with genius in there, and art, and music, and all the beautiful things. When a spirit person comes to earth and manages to stay tapped into that, he draws forth what is already existing. Gifted people can do that, beyond time in this one Collective spirit."

In deference to her daughter's spiritual journey perhaps, Natalia's mother created an alternative image of Creation and connection, one that still offered peace and eternal loving interaction. By avoiding the word 'God,' which can be loaded with unpleasant or even frightening weight for some people, this spirit mother found a way to guide her daughter through tragedy.

***

During a private reading for two women, another message about God came through via loved ones in the spirit world. Both Doris and Sherry were eager to connect with their people in the afterlife, and were happy to validate just about anything I said. Eager clients are a joy to work with, though sometimes I find it necessary to reign in the enthusiasm. If I begin with one characteristic, such as, "I have a woman in spirit who smoked," the enthusiastic client may interrupt with "Yes! That's my mother!" If it is indeed that client's mother, I'll get a *zing!* feeling right up my spine. If the connection isn't accurate, it feels as though I have a puzzle piece that won't snap into place.

After a couple of enthusiastic but incorrect exchanges with Doris and Sherry, I asked everyone, spirit people included, to take a step back and let me handle one long string of information at a time.

I then turned to Sherry with a woman in spirit. "She's indicating a pain in her head, which is a symbol of a stroke, and shows me the word 'mother.'"

"My mother's in spirit, but she didn't pass from a stroke," said Sherry. "It might be my grandmother, but I don't know how she passed."

I went back to the lady in spirit and asked for more.

"Do you know what a layette is?" I asked Sherry.

"Yes, for babies," she said.

"She's standing here holding her arms out and there's something in them. I'm asking her, 'What is it?' and she says 'It's a layette.' Do you have a baby blanket or baby table from her?"

"From my mother?" Sherry asked.

"Yes," I said. "Or from her mother?"

"Could be. But my mother's never told me, 'Here's something from your grandmother.'"

"She's showing me where a baby would lie down and be dressed," I continued. "I don't know what a layette is, but when I asked her she said, 'It's a layette.' She is making a connection. She wants me to talk about this because you will be able to connect it to her. Is there anyone you could ask about this? She is being quite specific!"

"I could ask, but what I know about my grandmother would not coincide with this," said Sherry.

We kept trying to give this to Sherry, but it seemed increasingly like a puzzle piece that didn't fit. The spirit was eager to make the connection, but instead of giving me additional information, she just kept showing the word 'layette,' over and over again.

Finally, Sherry's friend Doris said, "What about this layette?"

"She's showing me two things," I said, "and I'm trying to make sense of them. When I ask her, she shows me one and then the other. She shows me that she was a devout person; she is someone who prayed, and God was a big part of her life. She offers this layette, as if she's bearing gifts. She wants to give a gift to a baby, or she gave a gift to a baby."

"It has to be my godmother," says Doris.

"Do you know this lady in spirit I've been describing?"

"It's my godmother, I'm sure of it," Doris replied. "She had a stroke. And that's what she did. She would make every baby a baby blanket."

"Oh, my Lord!" said Sherry. "Why didn't you say anything?"

"Because she was talking to you!" was Doris's reply. "And I had that layette."

"Okay," I said, showing as little exasperation as possible. "Well, she's here."

"I loved her very much; I was very close to her," continued Doris.

"So this is why she's here bearing gifts. Was she a devout person when she was alive?"

"Oh, yes."

"There's a message she's giving about God," I continued, grateful to have made the connection. "She may have believed fully in one path or channel to get to Heaven, and maybe even went so far as to exclude or condemn other paths. Now in Heaven she understands it doesn't matter how you practice, what matters is that you believe."

"She was a Christian woman and critical of other religions," said Doris.

"Doris," I said, "you are experiencing psychic events now."

"Yes!" she replied.

"Your godmother wants to say, 'Don't confuse what a religious doctrine says about psychic ability with what is happening with you.' She's acknowledging your ability. It doesn't matter what you practice, what matters is that you believe. This is important and she's stressing the fact."

"I have a hard time connecting what's happening with good things," said Doris. "I always thought it was evil."

"Your godmother shows me what is psychic is natural, even though she didn't believe that when she was alive," I said. "God is available on all levels, in many ways. It's we who limit ourselves, not Him who limits us."

The subject of how God feels about how we worship Him comes up infrequently from the spirit people, but in each instance the message is the same: He loves us, and there is no right or wrong way to worship or believe. Usually this message comes through for a client who has strayed from his religious upbringing, or for a client who is interested in exploring the sixth sense, past lives, or alternative belief systems. Many who choose a different path struggle with feelings of guilt or doom, and seriously question whether they're diminishing their chances of getting to Heaven or even risking eternal Hellfire. It's always a comfort to deliver a message from a God who says, "Explore! Whatever brings you closer to a sense of awe is good! Whatever compels you to act more like Me is good!"

One client of mine received such a message and asked that if I were to include it in any of my books I keep only to the message and omit any personal details. He does allow me to say that the message came to us from his father in spirit during an individual reading. The spirit father had a rather funny way of speaking, but it was so charming I offer here a direct quote from the recording, grammatical inaccuracies and all:

"It's not so much *whether* you practice [faith], it's that you believe. Faith, believing, having a connection [to God] – doesn't matter the mechanics of your belief, the structure upon which you hang your faith, but only that you have the faith. Resting in the knowledge that there is something larger than yourself, or rely on the knowledge, is the point. It's not for God, it's for us. It's for you, here, that we have that. God isn't offended if you don't pray or believe in Him. It's for you people here so you can have some rest."

About Faith and Prayer

Faith and the practice of faith concern both my living clients and those in the spirit world. Many people feel that their faith is the right one, the best one, or the only one. Despite such certainty while living, those in the spirit world affirm that there are many paths to God, and that faith by its nature applies uniquely to each individual.

Marlena's mother had a rigid definition of faith when she was alive, so when she came through with this message, my client found it hard to believe.

"There's no way my mother is relaxed about religion now," Marlena insisted. "She always used to say, 'The only way to Heaven is through the Church.'" She went on to define her mother as an extremely conservative Christian, and expressed surprise that her spirit mother would even show up at a mediumship event, as she was opposed to psychic phenomena when she was alive.

"This is pretty common," I replied. "Once we get to the afterlife we understand physical life differently. There's no judgment in Heaven; that's what spirit people tell me over and over."

"That's the opposite of what my mother told me my whole life!" laughed Marlena. "Heaven is all about judgment!"

"Now she says this: 'My faith was a handle; I could hold onto it as I made my way through life. I realize now that the handle itself has no value unless it's attached to something. The real strength is where it is attached. It doesn't matter what the handle is. Whether you go to church or you don't go to church, whether you pray to a saint or not, the handle is just what people use if they want to or feel they need it. The handle itself isn't where worship belongs.'" I felt the power of that message as I translated it. "Your mother shows me how important faith is, but only if it adds value to your life."

"How is that different?" she asked.

"Faith is something you have, not something you do. Practicing a religion is something you do, and that can enhance faith or it can detract from it if you have a negative experience in a church. 'Practicing faith' is the ideal situation, but *doing* doesn't substitute for *having* if faith is absent from the practice. Does that make sense?"

"Yes, I think so," Marlena said.

"Your mother shows me she had faith, which morphed over time into a religious practice, and eventually overshadowed it," I said. "She felt lost from faith, so she grabbed harder onto the practice. It was from a feeling of insecurity. She understands now that retracing her steps and focusing on faith would have been better for her and her family."

"I see what you mean."

"So, from your mother's point of view now in the spirit world, she wants to encourage you to have faith if it gives you comfort, peace, or strength."

"But she's not telling me I'm going to burn in Hell if I don't go to church, right?" asked Marlena, only half joking. "Because that's what she used to tell all of us."

"No," I answered, "she's not telling you to go to church. What she is saying is to use faith as a handle to help you in tough times, keep you steady as you go forward, or rest on when you feel tired in life. It's a tool. But also remember to focus on or worship what you have faith *in*. That's where the real power lies."

"Even if that faith is in me?" she asked. "If I don't believe in God or a church, but I have faith in me?"

"Even if what you have faith in is you," I answered. "The level of your belief in God is not the measuring stick by which He loves you. She tells me it doesn't matter, just that having faith can be a real aid in life."

***

Another spirit person came through for my client Debbie, saying: "There are many paths to God. However you choose to practice faith isn't important, it's having faith that's important. Believe, even if it's to believe in yourself, or believe in your business plan. It's not so much how you believe; it's *that* you believe. Have faith, and make use of that faith, in whatever way feels most comfortable for you. There's only so much the mind can do, but we can invite in a higher Being, or have faith in a higher way of thinking. If we rely on or petition Someone wiser, we're going to have more to work with. We'll have more direction, comfort, and certainty in the way that we're supposed to go."

***

In an individual reading with Ellen, the spirit of a nun came through. She showed herself to be in a different country.

"I see a Spanish-speaking place," I said, "but not Spain. Central or South America."

"Okay, maybe...." said Ellen.

"She's wearing a rather old-fashioned habit," I said, "or at least she's stressing the habit to underscore that she's a nun. I see dozens of children around her. She may be a teacher. You two have an important relationship, she shows me, but you're not friends. Does that make sense?"

"Yes," Ellen replied. "My husband and I adopted a child from Bolivia. Nuns ran the orphanage. We dealt with one nun in particular, but it was so long ago I don't remember her name. This could be her."

"She wants to talk about faith. 'Faith should be easy,' she says. It should be natural. God is a person with whom we can be the most comfortable. We don't have to worry, 'I'd better pray this way,' or, 'I better be good,'" I said, not sure where the nun was going with this message. "God is Someone from whom you never have to hide. Let this be your easiest relationship, and let it be an example for the other relationships that you have. If something about you is changing, be comfortable first with God, and that will give you the courage and the confidence to be yourself and be comfortable with everyone else, just as you are."

"Oh, wow, that makes total sense to me right now," said Ellen.

"She's talking about accepting yourself as you are, that God meets you where you are, and then you can go out in the world and do the same – meet everybody else where they are and accept them. Go easy on yourself," I finished.

Ellen was particularly moved by this message because she had been struggling with the expression of her faith and feelings of guilt for deviating from her childhood religion. Her unsettled internal landscape had begun to contaminate her peace of mind and her other relationships, so hearing the message from a religious person was comforting.

***

Aline is an international phone client mentioned earlier in this book. During our first reading, a powerful and devout woman came in. Aline identified her right away as her great-grandmother, who was at the apex of the family tree.

"She wants to remind you of the power of prayer and that you can exercise the power of prayer without having to also fit into a religious doctrine that doesn't make you comfortable. I don't know why she's telling you this," I said.

"I know exactly why," answered Aline.

"You can call on God to help you," I continued. "She says, 'Don't forget the power of prayer. God is there for you and wants to lift you up.'"

"She was a religious woman," replied Aline. "She insisted the whole family pray together."

"There's a different energy about her in this communication," I said. "She doesn't seem to be insisting, but rather encouraging. She wants to say, 'Prayer works.'"

"I got away from prayer because it was forced on us when I was little," Aline said. "I didn't understand the purpose then, so it leaves a bad taste in my mouth."

"This message from her has love in it," I told Aline. "I feel no judgment in this, but she knows you might feel comforted if you try again, on your own terms."

***

Sue's Aunt Ann came in during a message circle, showing herself to be a devout woman by holding her hands in the prayer position.

"Your aunt tells me, 'This is the key to Heaven,'" I told Sue. "Earlier [in the message circle] I was talking about faith, but she is specifically showing her hands in prayer, and saying prayer is the key to Heaven. Whatever we wish for with fervency, desire, intention, and goodness, we are more likely to attract. She says this is the key to Heaven, here, on earth. If there is a Heaven on earth, prayer is the answer."

"I pray the regular prayers I learned as a kid," said Sue, "so I'm not sure what she means. More prayer like that?"

"My understanding of what she means is intentional visualization," I replied. "Intentional focus on your goal – wishing or praying – is going to set you on a trajectory of receiving, of being in Heaven on earth." Her Aunt Ann when on to affirm that prayer has many uses, and even if God doesn't answer our prayers the way we hope, He always hears us and always meets our needs. The spirit aunt encouraged Sue to pray for herself as well, which took some convincing as Sue felt it would be selfish to pray for her own happiness. She had been raised to believe that prayer should only be used for other people.

It's unfortunate that so many people struggle with faith and prayer. A relationship with God should be the easiest and most natural to retreat to, as Ellen's nun in spirit attested. Conflicting messages from human religious traditions complicate what could be the most rewarding and instructive interaction available. Spirit people always recommend that we relax in regard to the structure of faith or prayer and just begin to enjoy the closeness with God we all inherit.

Forgiveness and Following God's Lead

My client Maureen came in for an individual reading. I'd known Maureen for a couple of years and had done many readings for her and her sisters, but I had never met her Aunt Rose in spirit.

"There's a lady coming in now," I said to Maureen about halfway through our hour session. "She shows me a rose. I think she means to say she has a name like Rose." I reminded Maureen that I'm not clairaudient. If spirit people want to give me a name they need to show me an object or the face of someone I know, living or dead, with a similar name. Sometimes they'll even show me a saint of the same name.

"I have a Rose in spirit," Maureen affirmed.

"She practiced a traditional Christian faith when alive."

"She was a nun," said Maureen.

"She says when we're alive, we're not taught often enough to accept the fact we have been forgiven. We can put our mistakes behind us. She's asking me to tell you that you've already been forgiven for the past, and for anything you could possibly consider sinning about in the future. That's how much you are loved."

I noticed Maureen was tearing up, so I knew her spirit aunt was delivering an especially meaningful message.

"Traditional practice sometimes involved shame and exclusion if we didn't follow accepted dogma. Yet she tells me you are already known, you are already loved, and nothing you could do would separate you from a holy place to rest. We don't need to keep punishing ourselves; we can accept that we've been forgiven."

To this day I don't know what Maureen's Aunt Rose was referring to in particular, as Maureen didn't fill in any of the blanks for me. Whatever her aunt in spirit told her struck such a positive note, because my client never looked more peaceful or calm.

***

Another wondrous example of God's eternal partnership with us came from my client's older sister in spirit. After identifying her clearly through the visual and feeling evidence she gave me, the sister began to teach my client and I about balance.

"Your sister's message is, 'Forget about balance,'" I said, after we'd been discussing spirituality with her for about forty minutes. "You're already in balance. Thinking you have to use the mind through the body to create balance is a misuse of the mind. Does this make sense?"

"I'm not sure," my client answered. "I have been looking for balance in my life, but I don't know if that's what she's talking about."

"She is anxious that you don't waste time. She wants you to use your creation-ability with much more discernment. I was going to say 'creativity' but your spirit sister corrected me. You're trying to use your creation-ability to seek who you already are, the whole and divine spirit she was talking about earlier. You don't need to reinvent the wheel."

"I'm not sure I know what you're saying," said my client. "I think I do, but can she show me a different picture?"

"You're using your mind to perfect your spirit, and she says this is an unnecessary use of your mental creation-ability," I said. "You only need to follow God's lead."

I could see by my client's expression that she was trying hard to make sense of this message, as was I. We could both *almost* grasp it, but some key piece was missing that would allow her to integrate this message into her rational mind. I returned to the sister in spirit and asked for clarification once more.

"She shows me another way to get this point across," I said. "You know those old-fashioned dance instructions that show just the shoe prints, so you know where to move your feet?"

"Yes," my client laughed.

"Your sister says, 'You don't have to study these shoe prints,'" I said, the full impact of this message finally dawning on me. "She says, 'The one who's leading you – God – has that memorized and knows the dance, and you just have to follow.' You don't have to figure out, 'Does this move make sense?' and, 'Where do my feet go?'"

My client was paying close attention to what I was saying, and I knew I needed just one more explanation from her sister in order to complete this message. I asked the spirit sister, who responded in my mind with an additional impression.

"Okay, I think I finally get what she's trying to say," I said after pausing to digest this translation. "She shows me you have been thinking a lot about the need for balance or bringing more balance into your life. Instead of doing something like analyzing how you can make changes in your spirit or 'develop' your spirit, she wants you to recognize that mental effort isn't needed there. God is leading you; you don't have to make changes or decisions about your spirit. Let go of analysis there and turn it to what you can change in the physical and mental world. Let yourself be led by your spirit, rather than thinking you have to lead your spirit. God is showing you the way to go, just follow. That's what she's saying."

"I believe I understand this now," she replied. "I'm going to have to listen back to this recording a couple of times to get it."

"She's showing me one more example using the metaphor of a dressmaker's pattern pinned to fabric. She shows me shears cutting the fabric. The pattern is already there; you just have to follow the lines. There's no analysis you need to do on your own. You don't need to figure anything out. God will call you, and the correct response is to follow."

"Like I'm trying to train my dog to do!" laughed my client, who has a German Shepherd dog as I do. "I want him just to follow my commands, not think about it and decide whether it's right for him."

"Yes, exactly!" I said. "Smart dogs want a reason to cooperate, or they want to know what's in it for them. You can see them thinking about whether or not they want to come when they're called. In situations where they may get in trouble, it's important that they *not* think, and just follow."

We continued to talk about this important message for quite some time after our appointment was officially over. We agreed that God may always be calling us and that our lives would probably proceed much more smoothly and safely if we'd just follow.

I can think of many times when I was called to be compassionate, tolerant, and forgiving, but part of my mind first wanted a reason. For example, I once gave a presentation at a local middle school about the power of positive thinking. As one among many at the school's health fair, I taught fun self-hypnosis techniques and gave each child a free CD with audio files promoting good study habits, healthy self-confidence, and better sports performance. The superintendent told me later that one parent complained vehemently about my presence at the school. She thought hypnosis was dangerous, and she demanded that I never participate in the health fair again.

Not one year later this same woman came to me for help getting her permit through the municipal boards. Here was a perfect example of God calling me to follow Him to forgiveness, yet my own mind demanded, *Why? Why should I help this person who went out of her way to try to damage my reputation?* In this case, instead of forgiving or confronting her, I simply avoided the woman until she finally asked someone else for help. With the message my client's sister in spirit shared, I, too, learned about following God's lead. In hindsight, had I forgiven the woman for fear born out of ignorance about hypnosis, I would probably have enjoyed a spiritual and physical balance. As it was, I grumbled about that *imbalance* for quite some time.

What Heaven Feels Like and Life Between Lives

"What is Heaven like? Where exactly is the afterlife? Are all spirits together there?" These questions come up in almost every circle and reading. Just the other day, one of the guests in a large message circle demanded to know where her sister actually *was*. She was clearly able to identify her sister in spirit, but she couldn't understand why her sister did not bring every other family member who had passed in recorded memory. And, as her sister had known some of the other deceased whose family members were gathered at this circle, why hadn't she seen everyone who was here and gone to retrieve all of *their* beloved deceased, as well?

Despite my attempts to answer her questions, my guest wouldn't be mollified.

"I *know* it's her," she claimed. "She keeps showing me things to validate her presence, and they all make sense: the triangles, the paintings, the frogs, the irises..." This sister in spirit wanted to make darn sure her sister recognized her by coming through with almost a dozen unique identifiers. "But why isn't she bringing in other people?"

"I don't know," I answered simply and honestly. "I have no control over who comes in."

"But why won't she tell me more important things? Can't you ask her? All she's doing is saying who she is, but she isn't saying anything else," my guest replied.

"I don't know," I answered again. "I can no more explain her intentions or motivation than I can a living person's." I indicated another guest seated at the circle. "I don't know what Ella here is thinking, or why. I can't explain her actions, I only know what she tells me."

"Well," my guest continued, "she knew Ella's mother who's in Heaven. Why didn't my sister go get her? Can't she see us all here and say, 'Oh, let me go get Ella's mother, too'?"

"I don't know!" I repeated. "We don't know what Heaven is like. Spirit people have shown me different symbols for the afterlife. I don't know if the images and feelings they offer have to do with satisfying the client's expectations or if that's indeed what they're experiencing."

"Yes, but are they *together?*" she asked me. "You keep jumping from one spirit person to another, so obviously they're here side by side."

"Well, not necessarily," I answered. "Remember, Heaven may not be a physical place like earth is. We've already learned there's no time there, not in the same way that time exists here. Winnie's brother-in-law showed us that."

Earlier in the same message circle another guest's brother-in-law, Paul, had come in and stood before his niece, Winnie's daughter. Paul indicated that he had seen Winnie's daughter caring for his young children after he passed many years ago, and then began to describe how he continued to experience this in Heaven.

"I'm a little confused by what he's saying," I laughed, "so stay with me as I work this through. Your uncle shows me that he watched you play with his children and care for them right after he died. He's running a movie reel of one time in particular when you played with them in the pool. He runs it over and over, but he's doing it to show me that even though this was many years ago for you, and maybe the details have faded in your memory, for him it's always right now.

"This is an interesting way he's showing me time in the spirit world. He says it doesn't exist there. Or it does, but it's more flexible. For him no time has passed since this scene. When he replays it, it's right now, and he gets to hear the laughter and splashing and he sees some real joy his kids had in the middle of their grief and confusion. You did that for them. It's such an important moment. You don't see the impact, but it was noted, enjoyed, and made continually present for your uncle in the spirit world. You all live without him, counting days he's been away and missing him, but for him everything enjoyable is at his fingertips simultaneously. I don't know if I explained that very well," I finished. When I looked up, I saw Winnie's daughter crying happily and hugging her mother.

I restated this explanation of flexible time for my unsettled guest in the circle, and suggested that perhaps space or location is like this in the spirit world, too. I don't know whether the spirit people don't define Heaven because we can't understand it or because no words can describe it. One day we'll all experience it, but in the meantime we have to take what the spirit people offer and accept that there will be some mystery about Heaven until we go out and see for ourselves. In the end, I was unable to answer my guest's questions about the motivations of her sister in spirit and the details about Heaven, though I hope the very fact that her sister came through so strongly will encourage her.

***

Another sister in spirit came through during a different message circle. She was easily identified by my guest.

"Can I ask her a question?" asked Breanne.

"By all means. You can always ask spirit people questions, you don't need me."

"But we need you to translate the answer!" piped in another guest.
"Not necessarily, but I get what you mean. What's your question, Breanne?"

"My sister was emotionally spent. So sad and troubled. Does she feel better in Heaven?"

"Your sister wants me to talk about a specific feeling. Have you ever been on a very high floor in a building, looked out the window, and felt as though you were as endless as the view? This is bliss, not fear or vertigo. When you look out over a broad landscape or a big vista from high up, you are rooted to the spot but boundless at the same time. You feel as far off as the horizon, like you're floating over the whole scene. Big and small at the same time."

"Yes, I just did that," said Breanne. "I was on the observation deck at the Empire State building last weekend."

"When I get lost looking out a window, being in that state of mind – that's specifically the feeling your sister is talking about. When you're gazing into the distance, when there's a feeling of being weightless. Everything appears surreal."

"Yes, I know," Breanne replied. "Sometimes I feel outside of myself."

"She says, 'That's as close a feeling as I can give you, of how I am now.'"

"Oh, that makes me so happy!" cried Breanne.

"I know exactly that feeling she's giving me," I said. "A few days ago I was walking my dog in the woods and I came out on an unexpected overlook. I was on an uphill path in the woods, and suddenly I came out of the trees and I could see the whole Hudson Valley spread out below me for miles. Being up high and having a stunning vista, I felt a part of everything, the way the earth breathes, the silence, and the perfection. You feel a part of it all, but separate at the same time; blissful, almost out-of-body. She says, 'This is what Heaven feels like.'"

***

In a slight twist, my client and I received another description of the afterlife from her beloved pet cat. When her cat came through, Karen was able to identify her easily by the markings I described and the name she gave me.

"Did she cross a rainbow bridge?" Karen asked, referring to what many pet owners believe to be the animal pathway from earthly life to the spirit world.

"Your cat gives me an image that Heaven is a reflection of what you expect it to be," I said. "She does that by showing me a bridge, and the reflection of a bridge, to say that the bridge itself isn't there, but the reflection is. She's indicating to me that if we expect that to be reflected back to us, that's what happens for us. Anything that we expect will happen for us when we pass away or cross over, that's what we experience. But it's not *really* there, not a physical thing that's there. More like a manifestation of the expectation. Your cat says yes, and no. She saw the reflection of it, but she wasn't conveyed in this way herself."

***

Another spirit person strove to convey the feeling of Heaven to my client in an individual reading. Caroline recognized her mother in spirit when she described her battle with leukemia and showed her connection to her granddaughter by name. The spirit mother noted that Caroline had been dwelling on the afterlife quite a bit since her passing, by indulging in overlong meditations and visiting mediums multiple times.

"I'm drawn to this other realm," said Caroline. "I could contemplate Heaven all day. I don't see that as necessarily positive; it's escapism."

"Your mother tells me anyone who has passed away and come back says, 'I didn't want to come back, it's so peaceful here,'" I said. "People who seek the Kingdom of Heaven first find bliss in meditation and in prayer, and don't want to come back and deal with the real world."

"So I'm getting a taste of my mother's peace?" Caroline asked.

"That's what she shows me!" I replied.

"That makes me feel better," Caroline said.

"Your mother says, 'You don't have to pass away to enjoy the serenity and peace,'" I continued. "When you gain the mindset they have, you're going to feel this way, too. She says the closest we can get to the Heavenly peace is in deep meditation. But you can't meditate all day."

"I know," Caroline sighed. "I just miss her so much, and I feel like we're together when I hear from her through a medium or when I let myself go into a deep meditation."

"So she's showing you and sharing with you the bliss of Heaven," I said. "But she also wants to remind you that you have to function here, too. Feeling connected to Heaven and God, yes, that's a rewarding feeling. But let the goal be to carry that peace within you so you know that whatever challenge you have is just going to be a blip in time or a small wave to ride."

***

My client Ainsley's grandfather in spirit was a farmer, and used his physical experience to describe his Heaven.

"Your grandfather says, 'All of what was wonderful about farming is what I'm experiencing now.' He is talking about constant regeneration in nature, and bringing up plants from seed. That relationship is what Heaven is like for him."

"My mother will be so happy to hear that!" Ainsley replied. "She always said Heaven would be like the farm for Pop."

"You are looking for Heaven, too," I said, to which Ainsley nodded. "He would say to get more of nature. You can go to a natural place when you need to simplify complex thoughts or distill a complex decision down to clear choices. He has wisdom, but not the smoothest delivery. Being in nature is the answer to what ails you."

For each spirit person I've met, I have a different description of Heaven. The one common denominator is the extraordinary feeling of peace and fulfillment. I often wonder, with spirits such as Ainsley's grandfather, if we are born into physical life with a memory of Heaven and try to recapture it by seeking out a similar environment. Or, if a particular experience in human life feels so close to perfect that we are ushered into this environment in the afterlife. For me, Heaven would be a bright, clear mountain ridge or a cool, deep lake in the New England woods with my dog and my loved ones.

***

Reincarnation is far too vast a subject to bring up in this book, but a couple of interesting messages from spirit people might add to our understanding of the afterlife.

On more than one occasion I've seen spirit people who didn't make it into the world insist they'd be trying again. Many times I've seen spirit grandfathers or grandmothers holding little spirits who are waiting to come in, predicting pregnancy for a client or one of her family members. It's a great joy to take calls a few weeks later by excited clients saying, "My Grandma was right, I'm expecting!"

It wasn't until one peculiar episode during a message circle that I had a deeper glimpse into a way-station in the spirit world. On this occasion, I had an impression of a message, but not a description of the spirit conveying it. I searched for an identity but felt none, so I decided to proceed anyway.

Turning to one of my guests I asked, "Do you have an interest in medieval history, the Knights Templar, or Teutonic times?"

"I do," she answered.

"I never get this in message circles, so I'm just going to throw it out there. Do you believe in reincarnation?" I asked.

"I do," she replied.

"Did you ever have the sense that you lived in those times?" I asked, feeling a little silly. Personally I believe in reincarnation and have regressed hundreds of clients over the years. I've regressed myself with quite astonishing results. Having this topic come up in a message circle was out of the ordinary, however, as I prefer to connect with spirit people who can be identified.

"Yes, I do," she replied again.

"Someone is coming through with a sense that, 'Yes, you did.' This spirit is giving me the feeling that your sense about that is correct, that you were there, and that's why you have an interest in medieval times," I said.

The guest was looking at me expectantly, and so far no one had booed me out of my chair. I took a deep breath and charged on.

"I see a valentine. This symbolizes either a death in mid-February, or a sweetheart in the spirit world."

"Yes, in my previous life of medieval times," she answered. Now we were in unchartered territory for a message circle!

"This just gets more interesting," I said slowly, hardly believing what was transpiring. "You have a sweetheart from a past life, whom you've met in some of the work that you're doing now. I'm trying to unwind the threads that are running in my mind. Because I don't sense that this message is issuing from a *person* in the spirit world, though the message comes from there." This was getting weird. "It almost seems that someone left a message for you."

"My impression of it is that I'm aware of him, from the past. I've uncovered memories of that," she said.

"You recognize him here, in this life." I said.

"There is somebody that I've met in this life, who I believe is my sweetheart from the previous life," she answered. I was starting to see why I couldn't identify a spirit person. He wasn't fully in the spirit world; he was here, in physical form!

"My impression is that you're correct about living before, and you're correct about recognizing him from before. I'm not sure specifically who that's coming from, but if you continue to pursue this thread, you'll continue to validate your own impressions. Your own assessment of this development is correct."

After this unusual occurrence, I began to ask more questions of the spirit people regarding their time in the afterlife. Many clients who believe in reincarnation worry that by the time they go out, their loved one may have come back in and they'd miss each other in Heaven. With each client query, I began to formulate a picture of at least a certain section of the spirit world. According to the anecdotal evidence I've gathered from many circles and readings, spirit people seem to leave a part of themselves in the spirit world when they are born into human bodies. Perhaps this is what philosophers and spiritual teachers refer to as the Higher Mind. Maybe it's the part of us that makes up the Collective Unconscious. It could be the conscience, or even the part of us that we consider a Spirit Guide.

Heaven, the afterlife, the spirit world, the Great Beyond.... No matter what you call it, until we get there ourselves, it will remain a mystery. And what a mystery it is! Like a gripping Agatha Christie novel, we'll just have to wait till the end to see how it all comes together. And all of us will get to the end, because no "body" gets out of this alive. Let's enjoy life, forgive ourselves and others, follow our dreams, believe in ourselves, and open our minds to the benefits of ongoing communion with our beloved friends and family in the spirit world.

Meditation to Connect with Your Loved Ones in Spirit (16:34)

In this meditation, you might feel that your loved ones are around you, or you might have a visual impression. Maybe you'll hear a familiar voice, or smell a perfume, cigar, or cooking aromas. Let yourself enjoy these impressions. Remember, these sensations will likely not feel as strong as actual sounds, smells, or sights. Spirit people give us impressions in subtle ways, and they always tell us, "If you think it's me, you're right." Feel free to adjust any of the wording to suit you. Remember the keys to successful self-suggestion:

Every time you pay attention to an idea on purpose, with intention, it gets easier the next time. Repeat, repeat, repeat!

Use different images every time if you feel like it. There's no need to rigidly adhere to the same suggestions.

If something in this meditation doesn't quite resonate with you, tweak it. You must speak to your own subconscious mind in language or with examples you find believable or acceptable.

If you'd like to, record yourself reading this script. Be sure to make any adjustments you feel will suit your personal goal. Otherwise, have a general understanding of the path this script takes and recreate it in your mind. The words are not magic; if you don't recall it exactly during your meditation, that's perfectly fine. If you prefer to listen to a free recorded version of this script, go to: *http://liveandlearnguides.com/specialbookoffer/*

Some days you'll meditate easily and feel terrific. Other days you may only be able to settle in for a few minutes. That's okay. Repetition is more important than depth of trance.

Plan a time to do this. When we tell ourselves we're going to do something, we are more likely to follow through. It may help to set up a regular session so your loved ones in the spirit world can work with your rhythm, too.

Turn off any devices that might interrupt you and settle into a comfortable position. If you tend to fall asleep easily, try sitting up the first time.

You are now using your mind on purpose, to exercise your natural extrasensory communication skills. It's not necessary to be a professional medium to connect with your loved ones. They are trying to connect with you. Decide now that you'll accept them in whatever loving way, at whatever volume, they can visit. Each time you practice, your connections will be stronger because your loved ones in the spirit world will be practicing, too. They'll understand your attempts to reach them and will work with you to create a strong connection.

*Get comfortable, close your eyes, and begin to pay attention to your breathing. Breathe in and out as you normally do. By paying attention to your breathing, you naturally become aware of **how** you're breathing, so simply observe that. Imagine when you breathe in how your lungs gather the oxygen from that breath and move it right into your blood stream. Every cell in your body is taking part in every breath you take in and breathe out. Tell yourself now that every breath out will relax you. It's safe to relax, healthy for both the body and the mind. Every easy breath in refreshes you, and every easy breath out relaxes you, more and more, as all distraction drains away.*

Imagine you're stepping into an elevator. If for some reason you are uncomfortable in elevators, pretend that this one is as large as a room, very comfortable and safe. Imagine yourself stepping into this private, comfortable, safe elevator and locating the panel near the door. On this panel are buttons numbered from 1 to 10. As you step into this elevator and think about this panel, you notice that the number 1 is lit up from behind. Reach now, in your mind's eye, and push the number 10 button. See or imagine it lighting up now.

However you want this elevator to be, think about it now. Look around it or create it in your mind. Some people like glass elevators, where they can see the landscape spread out around them as they rise. Others prefer a luxuriously appointed cozy space, with comfy lounge chairs and beautiful music playing softly in the background. If you're one of the people who likes to have an elevator operator opening and closing the doors and operating the levers to get you to your floor, imagine him or her now, quietly following your request to go to the 10th floor.

Get comfortable for this ride. Sit down. Stretch out. This is going to be very, very relaxing.

Think about the elevator starting to rise now. As it moves from Level 1 to Level 2, tell yourself that you're temporarily leaving behind all of your cares and worries, your entire To Do list, mental projects and physical discomforts—all being left on the first level. Imagine your expectations being left there, too. Don't worry; when you return to this level you can pick them up again, or even leave them for the staff to gather up and discard. All of your baggage will be safe there.

As you approach the second level, you are dropping away—just for now—all distractions and disruptions, allowing you to focus and concentrate on the very special journey you're on.

See the Number 2 button light up on the panel as you pass this floor. Still rising at a very comfortable and safe pace, you begin to feel a deep relaxation spread through your body—as though you're leaving the force of gravity behind as you rise. Your body feels increasingly calm and relaxed, maybe even weightless or numb. Shoulders, neck, jaw... all relaxing more and more. Back, belly, chest... so comfortable. All of your organs functioning perfectly in a state of relaxation and good health. Your hips, legs and feet relax and let go, every nerve, muscle, tendon, bone and cell... relax and let go.

Now as you approach the third level, you may even experience yourself spreading out, softening around the edges. Maybe you begin to feel your edges expanding or blurring a bit, the way an ice cube melts and spreads. Think about your wonderful energy, your wonderful self, naturally and easily taking up a little more space.

See the Number 3 button on the panel light up, and imagine yourself expanding.

Every breath out continues to relax you, and brings you gently and safely out of conscious association with the body, and into conscious connection with your higher mind.

See the 4 button light up on the panel now. Imagine you are high above the earth, so if you were to peek out you'd see half the world below you, the curve of the far edge of the planet. Twinkling lights from the cities, lines of car lights moving like blood pulsing through veins. Very safe, very comfortable, very, very calm. You are open to whatever this experience brings you; you have left your expectations behind, and you give yourself permission to accept whatever comes to you.

Imagine now that the 5 button on the panel illuminates. You're half way there. You never felt safer or more imaginative or more relaxed than you feel now. Your energy is taking up its natural place in the world—an ever-expanding self that is connected to everything above and below. Like a vapor or a soft cloud, growing and moving, uncontained and uncontainable. You may even have a sense that you can look down at yourself now, resting here. You know on all the levels of your mind that you are completely and totally safe, and that your body is reverting to the healthiest it's ever been.

The 6 button lights up. Still rising, imagine you feel a growing weightlessness, or dissociation from your body. Imagine you can look out and see the earth far below you, and if you focus you can see a strong, unbreakable cord from you—where you are now in your mind—to your body and your home far below. Breathing naturally and normally, every breath out relaxes you more and more, expanding your ability to imagine and to trust that imagination.

Seven. Allow yourself to feel a growing anticipation, butterflies or a kind of excitement, as you are about to reunite with best friends and loved ones. What an exciting and happy reunion that will be. You will recognize your dear ones and you will be recognized by them. What a joyful, hearty greeting you can expect. Breathe, relax, look forward.

The 8 button lights up now as you feel the elevator begin to slow down. Look outside: all around you there are stars. You're deep in a star forest: stars above you and below you, on either side, beautiful, perfect, silent stars. Tranquility, serenity, peace. You are here: perfect, whole, complete, and beloved. One with this living, breathing universe: part of it and all of it at the same time. Imagine you can feel the timelessness of this place. Breathing in perfection, you breathe out disbelief.

Somewhere, in the back of your mind, you become aware of passing the ninth level, still rising, expanding, reconnecting and recovering your birthright of total joy, peace and love. What a happy moment! A moment that continues on and on for all eternity. You belong here.

Now, 10. The elevator has faded away, but waits for you where you can find it when it's time to return.

Take a moment to settle your awareness. You might want to look—with your eyes closed—at a point somewhere between your eyebrows, or at some other imagined place. Keep your focus here.

Now, very gently, check in with the energy on your right side. Imagine you can feel a presence there, or approaching you there. Don't question yourself, just allow yourself to feel as though someone very respectful comes towards you. Answering with the first thing that comes to mind, ask yourself—does this someone feel male or female? Trust your first instinct, just go with it for now.

Some people have a visual impression, some seem to hear the information, still others feel it come in the same way an idea pops into the mind. Let it be how it is for you. The more you concentrate, the more often you come here or the longer you stay, the more quickly and easily you will trust your own senses and the information that comes through. Let yourself once again check in with the energy on your right side. Does it feel male or female? Whatever seems to be the loudest, or brightest, or whatever seems to stick—just go with it.

Stay focused with your eyes closed and your mind open, just as you are now. Let more information come through from the being on your right. You may have an instantaneous thought pop into your mind that this is someone in particular, or it may take awhile for recognition to develop. That's okay.

Your mind may want to tell you you're making this up, but the spirit people always say, "If I pop into your mind, it's because I'm here," and "If you think it's me, it is." Trust that your sense of who might be beside you is valid.

Spirit people don't often use words, but convey their thoughts to us—which means greetings or messages from them can feel like we're just thinking our own thoughts or making up our own answers. Let the analysis go for now, just receive what your mind is making you aware of, and don't worry too much about the mechanics of how those thoughts got there.

You may want to ask if the spirit on your right is who you think it is. Offer a way for the person to say "Yes," by suggesting he or she give you a feeling. For instance, you can say, "If this is you, make my nose itch." If you are a visual person, suggest that an affirmative answer is a burst of color behind your closed eyelids. Or maybe you can ask to hear a certain sound in your mind's ear. It's a good idea to set up different sensations for different loved ones, so you will always know when they're around you – even when you're not in meditation.

Remember that their responses to you will likely be very subtle, and if you think you're feeling their presence or their "yes," choose to believe it, if only just for now. The more you practice this, the more fluency you'll experience.

Still focused on that point you're looking at with closed eyes, take a moment to feel or think about who may be on your left. Feel or imagine energy that is waiting there or that is approaching you. Is this energy male or female? Wait and see once again if recognition pops into your mind as you turn your attention to your left. Be patient. Both sides have to learn how to meet on the same frequency.

Now, look around you or think about looking around you with your mind's eye: is there anyone else there? Another person you know who has crossed over? You may find you're enjoying a quiet meeting with one or two loved ones, or you may find yourself in the middle of a big party of spirit people who have all come to greet you and reconnect with you.

Take a few moments to become familiar with the way you're feeling, with the energy of your loved ones, and with how information comes in to you. Each spirit person may feel different, or they may feel the same to you. Take your time. There is no wrong way to do this.

Do you have a specific question you'd like to ask one of these spirit people? Ask it now, and listen for the answer. Do you need help letting go of grief, or giving or receiving forgiveness? The spirit people have such great wisdom now. Would you like to know what the spirit world is like for them, or if they've seen another departed loved one? Maybe you'd like to know what they're doing, or if they can help send healing energy to someone here in the physical world. Ask whatever you like.

You'll remember everything you're experiencing. The spirits may answer you with direct information, or may suggest a way for you to discover the answer yourself. If you find that no answer is coming, ask your loved ones if they want you to know the answer now—perhaps part of your life plan is to discover the answer to this challenge on your own.

Now, turn your attention back to the spirit person on your right, and ask for a sign when he or she is near you. When you want to ask this spirit for help, or when this spirit wants to get your attention, let there be a signal of some sort that you can be aware of in your regular, waking state. Maybe it's an image of something, or maybe a feeling in your body. Perhaps you'll hear a buzzing or ringing in your ears. Is it the "yes" signal you got earlier?

Ask the spirit on your right for that signal now. Trust what you get, even if it feels slight. If you are feeling, hearing, seeing, or thinking about something, and you wonder if this is the signal, ask your guide now to confirm by making that feeling, image, sound, or thought brighter, louder, or stronger.

Now turn your attention to the loved one on your left side, and ask for a signal from him or her. It's likely to be different, so be open to a new impression. Take your time, double-check by asking again or by asking the spirit to intensify the sign.

All of your loved ones are here to support you. They are your support team on the other side. They may not always be able to get through every time, the instant you call them, but they want so much to help you, to remind you that everything is going to be all right. They know, and your higher mind knows, that everything will turn out okay, so you can be free of fear or worry or distress. You know that you'll all be reunited again.

Feel free to stay a while longer with your loved ones in spirit. When you're done, you'll be able to gently return to your five physical senses easily and quickly. If you intend to return to your waking state now, imagine stepping back into that elevator. Call it and have it appear before you, and settle yourself within it now. You can always return to this level whenever you want to. Reach in your mind's eye and push the number 1 button on the panel. Imagine the elevator begins to descend as you count yourself down from 10 to 1. When you reach the number 1, you'll open your eyes feeling wide awake and alert, and more confident than ever before in your ability to communicate with your spirit people.

PART THREE

"The grave is but a covered bridge,
leading from light to light through a brief darkness."
Henry Wadsworth Longfellow

Frequently Asked Questions

Over the years clients in message circles and individual readings
have asked me some probing questions. In fact, their questions have
helped me to define what I do more clearly, even for myself. I always
welcome inquiries about the process and experience of mediumship,
because I know that everyone is capable of spirit communication.
Part of my mission is to eliminate the fear and elitism that has thus
far been associated with mediumship. If you have questions for me
after reading this book, please just ask! You can send an email to
priscilla@apracticalpsychic.com. I will respond as soon as possible,
and if your question could enlighten others as well, I'll include it in
my ongoing list of FAQs on my website, and possibly in my next
publication. The following questions are in quotes because they are
taken directly from recordings.

Q: **"If you only see images or feel things, how do you get the
specific information like names? It sounds like you're relating the
words the spirit people are speaking to you, yet you say you can't
actually hear them. So how does that work?"**

A: It's not as hard to do as it is to explain. I suspend my personal
thoughts in fraction-of-a-second intervals (I'm no meditation guru)
and note the impressions that form. If you imagine talking without
thinking, or speaking the instant an idea pops into your mind before
your conscious mind has time to interfere, that's how I deliver messages.
Concentrating helps, as does closing my eyes. I don't hear the messages,
I just suddenly become aware of them. I start speaking and if I'm
sharing the impression incorrectly, the spirit will instantly stop the flow
and I'll feel as though I've forgotten what I was saying, mid-sentence.

I've learned that continuous talking helps because then my
conscious mind is too busy to interfere. I try to feel blank inside,

without thoughts of my own, without following any threads of my own devising. Just a blank state. That's hard for me to maintain for very long, though I work diligently on it. I think it gets better with practice. I never used to know what self-help teachers meant when they said, "Get out of your own way," or, "Make your mind blank," but I think I'm finally getting it. I think they mean, stop analyzing and have the experience without judgment. Say what comes into your mind.

I just had a circle last Thursday where I actually had to tell a guest to stop shaking her head. It was driving me crazy! I was starting to share some general impressions I had first, which is how it always happens as I warm up. I was telling her about a man who had trouble breathing, and she was shaking her head. I said, "Stop shaking your head! You're not going to hear what I'm saying if you're already rejecting it." She was quite startled. But it was interfering with my ability to get out of my way, because my conscious mind jumped in to tell me I was failing, and that's the kiss of death (no pun intended) when I'm trying to deliver a message or impression.

I'm a frequent guest minister at a Spiritualist Church in Connecticut, and part of the service includes spirit communication. A short while ago I was giving the spirit communication, when a picture of early space travel came into my mind. I thought, *No way. No one here in this church has anything to do with the space program.* I tried to squeeze that image into a message about adventure. Thankfully one of the ladies in the congregation said, "Everything you're saying is correct... and my friend was the first woman to work in the space program." If I had only spoken freely about the image I'd had, without letting my own rational mind get in the way, I would have delivered that much more succinctly.

I can also compare the experience of accurate mediumship to free-association. An image triggers an idea or thought or impression, and I say it immediately without judging the content.

Q: "How do you reconcile your belief that there is no evil with a long history of possessions?"

A. As for the long history of possessions, I think the human mind is capable of extraordinary things, and I also think the power of suggestion is far more powerful than anyone gives it credit for. Hopefully, I won't be tested in this regard. But, like curses, I feel if you don't consider evil an option, it won't be a possible outcome.

I remember mountaineering in Washington with a friend who was as much of a beginner as I was at the time. We were coming down from our first climb together and had achieved the glacier, which didn't appear to be too crevassed. We could see every gaping crack in front of us, so we felt secure enough to unrope from each other. (I learned in subsequent expeditions that just because you can't see a crevasse doesn't mean it isn't there.)

We each carried a rope on our pack. I was ahead of her, she was behind and to my left. I heard her shout and suddenly she was tumbling past me. Rhonda was almost completely round: short and thick in the middle, and she was literally rolling past me. Further down on the glacier there was a huge crevasse, and Rhonda was sliding and bouncing toward it in an uncontrolled fall. Everything seemed to slow down. I think I had enough time to calculate that if she fell into that thing – and survived – I didn't have enough rope to get her out. Right at the last minute she bounced up onto her feet and leapt perfectly and gracefully over the crevasse. She never could have done it standing still, but she had enough momentum so when she tapped her foot she sailed right over it.

I don't know how she did it, but I was glad she'd made it. After we both had recovered our senses – and roped up again – I asked her what was going through her mind, and how she managed to get ahold of herself right at the lip of the crevasse. She told me in a perfectly calm voice, "Falling in was not an option." That was about twenty years ago, but I have never forgotten it. For Rhonda, falling into a bottomless crevasse was not a possibility worth considering, even as she was falling toward it. She held just one outcome in her mind, and her experience obeyed.

It's the same thing with evil. For me, it's just not an option. If the thought even tickles at the edge of my mind, I jump all over it and kick it right out of my thoughts, immediately filling that space with different thoughts. And thus far, my experience has obeyed. This matches my growing spiritual awareness that only Love exists, and what we may consider to be evil is just perceived distance from that Love.

Q: "Does anyone ever come through for someone else who is waiting for a reading?"

A: All the time! Two friends came to my home together for individual readings. Tori came with me into my session room while her friend waited out in the living room. We'd been talking with her mother in spirit, whom Tori had easily identified.

"I see wings. Are you into angels or butterflies?" I asked. "Do you have a tattoo with wings or are you thinking about getting one?"

"Ummm, no, not really," she answered.

"I'm asking because there's a woman in spirit here showing me a picture of wings, not wings itself. Not an actual butterfly wing or a feathered wing like an angel would have, but a picture of it. Is that relevant to you in some way that you can think of?" I asked.

"No," Tori replied again.

"Are you into angels or birds?" I tried one more time.

"No, not in particular," she said.

"Let me look a little more closely at this, because she's showing me wings, a picture of wings, and at first it went from a butterfly to a bird wing and back to a butterfly. So she wants me to talk about wings. I sense that it was literal, but if it doesn't have a literal meaning for you I'm going to go with what I do next, which is go to the symbolic meaning...." I waited in vain for the symbolic meaning to appear. "No, I'm not going to do that," I laughed, correcting myself. "She shows me that she has, or you have.... do you have a necklace with wings on it, a piece of jewelry that has a butterfly or angel wing on it? A picture or a symbol of an angel that's connected with her?"

"Would this definitely be with my mother?" asked Tori.

"Not necessarily," I said. "There could be another person joining us here. Is there another person in the spirit world that you would connect this to?"

"Not for me, but it would be for Jackie," said Tori, referring to her friend waiting out in the living room.

"Jackie's people could be here already. Okay, I'll ask this spirit person to wait outside until we're done here, and I'm sitting with Jackie," I said.

Tori and I concluded our session, and I walked her out to the living room. I wanted to make sure that I could bring Jackie right in before any information passed between the two friends.

Sitting with Jackie for her private session, I brought in her mother in spirit. Her mother described her personality and her genetic heart condition, which Jackie acknowledged.

"What about the wings?" I asked.

"Everything!" said Jackie, who began laughing and crying at the same time.

"She could not wait to get here!" I said.

"She loved angels," Jackie replied.

"She also shows me a picture of wings. Did you get a tattoo? Or do you have a figurine or necklace with wings?" I asked.

"Yes!" she said, pulling out a necklace of angel wings and revealing an angel tattoo. Jackie's mother was so eager to get through she pushed her way into Tori's reading. Tori had met Jackie's mother and was fortunately able to identify her for her friend.

More recently I had another spirit person come in at the beginning of the day for clients I wouldn't see until later that day. For my first appointment of the day, I'd had a single client for a one-on-one reading. She was able to clearly identify both of her grandfathers, and our session went smoothly. Breaking in throughout the reading, however, was a young man who showed me a terrible head injury due to his own recklessness. He showed me coma or brain death, and then removal from life support. This young spirit man gave me the feeling of being in his mid-twenties at most, indicated a motorcycle, and claimed responsibility for his passing. I could even feel the tube in my throat as I tried to give him to my client Stephanie. She was unable to validate him, so I asked him to wait alongside me and only interrupt again if he could add information she would recognize. When our session ended without this young man reasserting himself, I concluded either I'd read him incorrectly, or Stephanie would recall him later on.

My next appointment was spirit communication for two sisters. Their dad came through, as did grandparents and a great-grandparent, all of whom the sisters readily identified. We were enjoying the reunion when I felt the brain dead young man again. "Aha!" I thought to myself. "He just came early, he wasn't for Stephanie at all, but for these ladies." Neither one of the sisters, both middle-aged women, could identify him. Our session ended without any of us being able to validate this young man's identity.

Finally, my last appointment of the day was a message circle in a town about an hour away. Eight guests were present, and we had a terrific time as the loved ones came through one by one, inciting laughter, happy tears, and meaningful, personal messages. I was just about to close for the evening when the young man in spirit came through once again. I thought to myself, *What now? Really? What the heck am I supposed to do with you?*

He marched right over to stand in front of one of my guests and nearly shouted at me to announce him. Wearily, I began again what I'd already described twice that day. This time, I hadn't gotten half a sentence out before my guest, a young man in his mid-twenties, buried his face in his hands and began sobbing.

It turns out this was his dear friend who passed away after being on life support for a couple of months. My guest had been hoping to hear from him and had been thinking about him all day. Apparently this spirit friend had been so determined to be recognized and brought through for his friend, he'd begun connecting with me early in the day.

Which now presents me with another system to set up. In the past I've had to set up filters or systems to screen spirit people for clients who work in hospice, emergency rooms, or cancer centers. Nurses and doctors touch many peoples' lives, and often those who have passed away want to come through and say, "Thank you." Unfortunately, not every doctor and nurse remembers every patient who has ever been under his care. Now I'll have to find a way to admit spirit people only for those present *right now*. As there's no time as we know it in the spirit world, I'm going to have to work with them to find a way to hold spirits for later clients back. Maybe I need a doorman with a velvet rope!

Q: "Sometimes you say very specific things from one spirit person, and other times you just describe the spirit person and you don't give a message. Why is that?"

A: I don't know. That's the honest answer.

Remember: I'm not creating this interaction, I'm reporting it. A spirit person may come through with a vague description of herself, just enough for you to recognize, and then pour most of her energy into crafting precisely the message you need to hear. Other spirit people will use their energy to define themselves to an exact degree, and stop there. Perhaps they only have limited energy to spend connecting with me or depositing impressions into my mind, and it may be more relevant that you know beyond a shadow of a doubt that this surely is your loved one. That itself is probably the message then, that this person, this man or woman who has died and gone out to the spirit world, is unquestionably here. I've seen that before: the message is, simply, "I'm here. I'm living."

Q: "Has anyone famous ever come through in a reading?"

A: Just a few times, and it took me a long time to admit they were here! There have been quite a few locally known people, and I responded the same way. For example, I had a client come with a friend whose husband was killed in a murder-suicide. It was all over the papers. While that didn't make the spirit people famous per se, their names and the cause of passing had quite a bit of local notoriety. When the husband first came through and connected himself to this horrific incident (he was the murderer and ultimately the suicide), I was reluctant to admit this to my clients. I constantly struggle to quiet down my conscious mind, which wants to either fill in the blanks

(*Oh, this must be the guy from downtown. Remember the details in the newspaper?*) or deny it completely (*You're totally making that up! You just read that in the paper!*). In cases like this, I ask the spirit person to present me with information unrelated to the famous details, information only the client will recognize. This spirit husband did so, was identified and validated through several impressions I shared with his wife. Only after she clearly validated her husband, did I admit aloud that I knew of him.

During one message circle I was holding at a new age center in another town, I became aware of a spirit man in an old-fashioned life jacket. He gave me the impression that he died on the Titanic. *No way*, I said to myself. *There's no way anyone here would be connected to that. They're all under forty!* So I carried on, giving messages to all the guests assembled. As the circle came to an end, all the gathered spirit people stepped back into the shadows, except for one. One lone spirit man in a life jacket stood in the middle of the circle, right in front of a young woman. *Well,* I thought to myself, *I've brought through quite a few people she was able to validate, and she appears to be satisfied that I'm not a fake, so, why not?*

"Carol?" I ventured.

"Yes?" she said, leaning forward in her chair.

"God, I can't believe I'm going to say this, but there is a man in front of you who went down on the Titanic," I sputtered, inwardly cringing.

"Oh, yes!" she cried. "I have an ancestor who died on the Titanic. We were doing our ancestry not too long ago and found that out."

Not exactly a famous person, but a famous ship! There is so much fraud in this business of spirit communication, I can hardly believe that famous people or victims of well-known disasters will come to me. They've gone out to the spirit world, too, and it's likely that living people can identify them. I hold those spirit people (and myself) to a higher standard when they appear, which may or may not be fair.

Finally, I had a family reading which was going along perfectly until Ray Charles showed up in spirit. Because I don't hear spirit impressions in my mind's ear, the spirit people will often show me the face of a celebrity or someone else I recognize in order for me to say a name. So when Ray Charles appeared in front of the father, Bruce, I asked him, "Can you connect to the name Charles?"

"Hmmm," he said, looking at his wife. "No, I don't think so." It's funny for me to watch husbands and wives together at message circles, because many times the wives know more about their husbands' families than the men do themselves. "Do we know a Charles, Honey?"

"Not that I can think of," she said.

"Okay," I said. "I have a person here who is showing me the face of someone I know in order to get me to say his name, so if it isn't Charles, do you know a Ray or a Roy?" I asked.

"No, no Ray or Roy either," they both said.

"Okay, I must be misreading this," I said, and continued on bringing through other spirits. At the end, when all the other connections had dissolved, I was face-to-face with Ray Charles in the spirit world.

"I still have this one man in front of me," I said, dismissing the unlikely possibility that this couple would know the famous musician. For Heaven's sake, they were a regular middle-aged couple from New Jersey, with regular jobs, kids, and a nice house in the suburbs. I asked the spirit-impersonating-Ray-Charles to *please* give me something else or I was going to close up and let him go. I felt a jolt of energy, saw both names, and felt as though the spirit underlined each one, firmly and deliberately.

With a sigh I said, "You know who I see? I'm trying to figure out who this is supposed to be. But I see Ray Charles."

"Ray Charles!" crowed Bruce. "My father was a producer and Ray used to come to our house when I was a little kid. I grew up loving music because of him. He was like an uncle to me. I saw him often when I was a kid, but after my dad died most of his old musician friends moved on. Wow, I can't believe he's here!"

I couldn't either, but I was certainly impressed with his persistence!

Q: "How exactly does symbolism work. You say you see symbols, but I'm not sure what that means, and how do you know what you're seeing is a symbol?"

A: I haven't figured it out entirely myself. Symbols aren't always the same. Because the spirit people aren't speaking directly to me, as you are now, they have to find different ways to get me to talk about things. If they want to talk about themselves, they can give visual or feeling descriptions. No symbolism needed.

If they're trying to get across a concept, state of mind, or anything else, they have to stir up an idea in my own memory bank. They'll poke around in my mind for an experience I've had that's similar to their information, then bring it to my awareness and say, "Reference this feeling." One spirit woman wanted to be defined in a particular way, so she presented my own long-dead grandmother as a symbol and I found myself recalling what my parents always said about her.

"She's describing herself, or as others would have. She shows me an iron fist in a velvet glove," I said, referencing what my parents always said about my grandmother.

"Oh, my God!" my client cried out. "That's exactly what she was, soft and sweet on the outside, but, man, she ruled the house with an iron will!"

In this case the spirit woman showed me my grandmother and unleashed a long-buried catchphrase I'd heard associated with her, but hadn't heard in decades. That was an efficient way for the spirit to convey her character. It would have been more tedious for both of us, and perhaps would have taken too much of her energy, to spell out her personality another, longer way.

I have reusable symbols, too. For example, if I see a cancer ribbon on its side it means cancer began in one place and spread to or returned in another. If I see a cross on its side, it means the spirit or the client has departed from a traditional religious practice. A bouquet of flowers represents an anniversary of a wedding or passing, or marks some other annual ritual. An owl is a symbol for the name Diane or Diana. A frog symbolizes global change in a person's life; swans swimming around the client represent physical healing. These I can rely on to be fairly consistent from one reading to the next, but everything else I need to interpret on the spot.

A woman came through in spirit for one of my guests, who was able to validate her ovarian cancer but not much else. I saw "two times" and also felt concern with her lungs. Then the spirit showed me a menorah, with all eight candles lighted. I focused first on the candles.

"Did someone light a candle for her?" I asked.

"I don't know," my guest answered.

"Did it take her eight days to die?" I tried. These eight candles were not going away. I looked again and waited. The candles didn't have anything to do with it. This was a symbol for eight days.

"I don't know. I was a baby," she said.

"I also feel Thanksgiving, does this make sense?" I asked.

"Wow, I don't know. I just don't know the answer to that," my guest replied.

While we connected other details to this spirit woman, the symbol of eight was unresolved during the message circle, as were a couple of other details. A week or so later I received this email from that guest:

"I just wanted to share with you something that I was completely unaware of, being that I wasn't very knowledgeable about my mom's father and my mom's sister. She was the woman you were connecting through to me with the ovarian cancer. I was unaware that she had both lung cancer and ovarian cancer. It spread from her ovaries to her lungs. Maybe that would explain the connection we were trying to make, and also when you mentioned the 'two times' of cancer. She learned she was cancer free in February, and by July or August she learned it came back. Also, the Connecticut connection we had mentioned, ended up actually being where she was born.

"You had also mentioned Thanksgiving being special for this person, and I was unaware but my aunt had passed away eight days before that and you said there was a connection with eight and Thanksgiving."

How do I know when an impression is a symbol? I wait. When I'm given an image in my mind's eye, I wait to see if a feeling follows. For example, the other day I saw my own Polish grandmother Joanna. That could be three potential translations: the spirit is making a connection to Poland, she's a grandmother, or her name resembles Joanne or Joanna. When this comes to me, I wait to see which translation fits best. That is, my thoughts keep returning to one aspect out of the three. Let's say it's Poland. I'll push back a little by trying to think more about grandmother or Joanna. If Poland is the correct thread, my thoughts will bounce back to the Poland feeling, like an elastic band snapping back. This all happens quickly, because I don't want to spend a lot of my time engaging my conscious mind. When I'm settled on one aspect, I would then say to the client, "I see a connection to Poland."

Or, I may see a train in my mind's eye when bringing in a detail about a spirit person. I'll wait a bit, and if the image of the train is not followed by a feeling or a memory, I'll realize that a literal translation is required. I would say, "He shows me trains, so he may have worked on the railroad or had trains as a hobby."

If I see a train in my mind and an instant later remember being in a Swiss train station, I realize the train is symbolic and would say, "He gives me the feeling he was punctual, always on time." Using a symbol I personally know to represent punctuality is an efficient way for a spirit person to share a unique characteristic about himself.

At times I'm not sure whether I'm dealing with a symbol or a literal translation, usually because I'm rushing, but sometimes because both apply. This most often happens with regard to names. During a large message circle in Brooklyn I became aware of an owl in front of one of my guests. We were already in contact with her aunt in spirit, so when I saw the owl in front of the guest I didn't bother waiting to see if the owl was symbolic or literal. "She shows me the name Diane or Diana," I announced.

"That's not her name," my guest replied. "I'm not sure who that is."

"Really?" I asked. I looked again and, still seeing the owl, paid close attention to the feeling I expected it to evoke. Nothing happened. No feeling, just picture. This wasn't a symbol for the name Diane or Diane, this was the image I was supposed to convey literally. *Dope,* I said to myself. *Slow down.*

"I mentioned the name because she shows me an owl," I said, "and I rushed to a conclusion."

"Oh, she loved owls!" cried my guest, not unexpectedly. "She collected them, she had dozens of them."

Of course she did, I thought to myself. I'm sure I'll continue to learn about symbols with each reading I do, if I can remind myself I don't know everything yet.

Q: "My dog barks at nothing or twirls in circles. Right after my dad passed he'd sit in front of his chair and bark at the empty seat. Is he seeing my father?"

Q: "My cat stares up into space at nothing and then he'll run off like his tail is on fire. Does he see ghosts?"

A: I happen to think that young children and animals see things adult humans don't. Animals in particular may pick up on the energy of a spirit person or even another animal in spirit.

Four years ago I began raising a German Shepherd puppy for Guiding Eyes For The Blind. Memphis came to my home at twelve weeks old, and for the next eleven months we took the weekly classes GEB mandated for their volunteer puppy raisers. Unfortunately, Memphis developed allergies and was released from the program at about a year old. As his raiser I was given the option to adopt him, which I gladly did. Ever since he was a puppy, Memphis has been present in my home during message circles and readings. He's learned to greet the clients peacefully and to lay down quietly for the duration of our sessions.

I was finishing a successful message circle with a group of five friends. Memphis was lying on his side at the edge of the room in a deep sleep, as he had been all night. My guest Marybeth had connected with many of her loved ones in spirit, and asked right before we finished if I could contact her beloved dog who'd recently passed. I closed my eyes and went looking. By that I mean I tuned out my five senses and concentrated hard on the black field of my closed eyelids, waiting for some feeling or image to appear. Before I long, I found myself in the company of a small white dog.

"I have a fluffy, light colored dog here," I said to Marybeth. "Small, shin-high maybe. A dog like a Bichon."

"Oh, yes, that's my girl Lola!" she said. "She passed away about eight years ago."

"This isn't the one you're looking for?" I asked, recalling that Marybeth had said her dog had passed away recently.

"No, Scarlett is a big black lab," she answered, before I was able to prevent her from volunteering information. Though it's hard to do,

I always ask my clients to try not to offer me any details about their spirit people. For example, if I say "I have a small white dog here," I discourage my clients from the natural inclination to help by saying, "No, my dog was big and black." Now that I knew the name and description of the dog she was looking for, it was difficult for me to determine if the things I saw in my mind's eye were spirit impressions or information from my thinking mind. I asked Scarlett, if she were out there and able to come in, to give me impressions I didn't know about her.

I waited and waited, to no avail. Finally, I said to Marybeth, "I'm sorry, I don't see her. That doesn't mean she isn't in the spirit world. The fact that Lola came through is a testimony to that. Maybe we're just not on the same frequency."

Marybeth looked so woebegone, I rededicated myself and went back in to search once more. With my eyes closed, I heard the women in the group start to whisper at the same time I heard Memphis get up. When I opened my eyes, Memphis was walking across the room until he stood in front of Marybeth. He pushed his way between her knees, stretched his neck up to lick her face, and then turned around and went right back to where he'd been sleeping a moment ago. He flopped down onto his side and promptly began snoring softly. I don't think he ever actually woke up.

We were all speechless as Marybeth whispered, "That's exactly what Scarlett used to do!"

Where I had struggled to bring in Marybeth's dog, Memphis had helped out. In this case, he may not have seen her, but he certainly seemed to be responding to a message she was trying to get through, a message I had been unable to present. Marybeth was sure that Scarlett had communicated with Memphis, and that her spirit dog suggested he perform an action I'd never seen him do for me or any other client.

While the honest answer is, "I don't know if animals see spirit people," I feel fairly confident that they do. And the spirit people always say, "If you think it's me, it's me."

Q: "I know you talk a lot about how we're already forgiven, and that there isn't any judgment in the spirit world, but I have a hard time believing it. I've done some things in my past that I'm so ashamed of, I can't believe I haven't ruined my soul completely."

A: This question came from my client Miles, an older gentleman who had been to see me a few times. His mentor Roger had come through quite clearly at the beginning of our reading and stayed by Miles' side throughout. Miles was questioning the existence of the afterlife, as many people do, so I felt that this was the reason his spirit friend Roger continued to present strong evidence of his identity. Usually spirit people will come in, establish themselves, be validated, give a message, and move aside so another spirit can come in. Roger wasn't going anywhere. Any time another spirit came in, he was allowed to establish his identity and then was were promptly booted to the back of the line by Roger.

"Roger's insisting on taking center stage," I said to Miles. "I don't see this too often. He doesn't want to share!"

"I guess he knows he's the only one I'd believe," Miles answered.

"What do you mean?" I asked.

"All these other people, I know who they are," he said, "but they weren't good people to me. Roger and his wife took care of me; they raised me. I have no faith in those other people."

"And so if it comes from Roger, you'll believe it?" I asked.

"Probably. It will still be hard," said Miles. That's when he asked me the above question.

"Well, let's ask Roger to answer this," I said, knowing that if the words came from any of the others or even from my personal experience about the spirit people, it would be insufficient for Miles.

"He shows me a vintage car," I said. "He was into cars, how they looked and how they ran."

"Yes, he was," answered Miles.

"He shows me caring lovingly for the cars, both the engine and the body," I continued. I waited and Roger, as I suspected he would, began to use this hobby of his as a message.

"Roger shows me a car that runs beautifully," I said, "but it has a few dings in the body. A couple of scratches or small dents, but the engine runs fine." Now I could see where Roger was going with this metaphor.

"He tells me that the spirit of a person is like the engine, and the habits, actions, personalities, and physical form are like the body. It's like aging. Over time, we're going to collect some scars and scratches, but those things only affect the shell."

"I see," Miles said.

Roger wasn't done. "He *fervently* wants to be identified!" I said laughing. "Do you believe this is him here with us?" I asked Miles.

"Yes," he said.

"Good, because he wants you to believe him. He knows what he's talking about," I continued. "You have to look at those past decisions, no matter how brutal or destructive they may have been, as only affecting the shell, the body of the car. Whatever you ran into or ran over, the engine is completely untouched. You can't degrade the engine at all, no matter what the body of the car looks like. Only the engine – the spirit – goes into the spirit world."

"I believe him," Miles said. "That's good to hear."

I know it can be hard to believe that we won't be punished eternally for past actions, but the spirit people remind us that judgment happens here during human life, and in the spirit world we can expect acceptance, welcome, and unconditional love.

Q: "How long are they able to speak? Is it the strength of the soul?"

A: I think it has to do with me and my frequency. Sometimes I'll meet with people I've had as clients before, and I'll bring through totally different spirits than those who came through the first time. Why a spirit comes through in one reading and not another, I have no idea. I've tried for years to figure it out, but I cannot find any common denominator or any particular key to why your mother would come in for our first reading, for instance, but not come in during our second one.

Spirit people have a lot more control over the situation than I do, which is why I say I have no control over who's going to come through. Sometimes it's a lot of work for me to bring messages through, and other times it's like water pouring through me. I have tried for fifteen years to control the reading, but the fact is sometimes I can give one strong, clear message after another, and other times I wait long minutes between hits. There are perfect moments when I'm spontaneously translating, with no rational mind interference at all. At these times unique names, characteristics, or messages come through fluently. I know how I feel at that time, but can't always create it on purpose. I used to spend time in meditation before readings, but because I do best when I'm not thinking about the process of spirit communication, I've had more success when I don't prepare at all! If I think too much about what I'm going to be doing, or if I pray too hard for success, I find my rational mind keeping track of how I'm doing, and that's a recipe for interference and missed translations.

Q: "If someone was normally quiet-natured in her life, would she have a harder time coming in?"

A: Not usually. She would establish herself first, and then indicate her quiet-nature. Simply being shy wouldn't affect her ability to connect with me. A spirit will give me that as a characteristic, but it won't necessarily determine the clarity of her contact with me.

Strength of personality does not automatically equate to strength of connection. I've had powerful, forceful, insistent connections from spirits who were timid and meek during their physical lives. I've also had very tenuous connections with spirits who were aggressive bullies in life. It's crucial for me to distinguish between the power of our connection and the personality of the spirit. It's also important to note that spirit people are highly unlikely to come through from the spirit world expressing current anger, hostility, or dismay. They may make me aware of that aspect of their human personalities, but we mustn't mistakenly assume they still feel that way now. I have never had a spirit person express anger or judgment from the spirit world – though they have referred to it as an identifying characteristic. All negative emotions are tied up in the ego and the human mind, and the spirits assure me that part dies with the body. Only love and understanding, which are bound up in the spirit, are eternal and persist into the spirit world.

Q: "Why does one come, and the others not? When one relative comes through, why doesn't he bring someone else with him?"

A: I don't know. Perhaps it has to do with who can match my particular frequency on any given day. That's why acknowledging every spirit is important. You might not have been close to boring old Uncle Joe, but I may need him to connect with somebody you *do* want to hear from. If one spirit doesn't accompany another, it doesn't mean they aren't together.

Also, just because spirits come through side by side it doesn't mean they are in the same location. Heaven seems to be non-local, so togetherness is an entirely different concept. Rather than thinking about spirit people as being in the same place when they come through, think of them as coming in at the same time. Think of a medium as an operator at an old-fashioned switchboard, receiving many calls simultaneously and putting them all through to you.

Q: "So they come in, they've shown all the signs, they're validated, they made a connection, why can't they say something about other people that would be important in their lives? My sister came in and spent all this time sending me signs that it was her, and I believe it. Why wouldn't she mention something about her two sons?"

A: The answer is, once again, I don't know. The spirit people don't always have a message, other than "I'm still here, I'm with you, I know what's going on in your life."

Remember, I'm just the interpreter. I don't know your spirit people, or what their motivations are for coming through or not coming through. Mediumship is not an exact science, and the afterlife is still far beyond our rational comprehension. We may just need to accept that some questions will remain unanswered until we go out ourselves. We may just have to accept the mystery.

Q: "When people are more open to the process or the medium, are their spirit people more easily channeled?"

A: Not necessarily, but it sure does make the client easier to work with!

I began a reading the other day by introducing a young man in spirit who died in a car accident around the age of twenty-three. My client couldn't identify him immediately so I asked the spirit for additional information. I delivered another symbol, but my client still couldn't identify him. She told me "No" for the second time. "He shows me the name 'Robert,'" I said, to which my client replied, "I don't know anyone named Robert."

I could see that she was getting into what I call the *No* cycle, so I introduced a different spirit man by name and cause of death. My client replied, "Nope, no, no idea." She was shutting herself down to the process with her repeated denials and risked missing the chance to connect with her loved ones. I asked her to take a deep breath with me and suggested she say "I'm not sure," instead of "No." Within minutes, not only could my client identify the second spirit – *her brother!* – but she was able to identify Robert as well.

This client came to the reading with an open mind but slipped into a *No* cycle that could have prevented her from hearing messages, though it wouldn't have prevented me from delivering them. We are all suggestible, and can shut ourselves down by repeatedly dismissing evidence the medium offers. That's not to say you must accept what you cannot validate. Good mediums work as much for the spirit person as for the physical person, and will guide you back to a more open state of mind.

I have had clients all along the spectrum of openness, from wholehearted acceptance to total opposition. The more skeptical are easy to identify: they'll sit with arms folded across the chest, or push their chairs back from the circle. I welcome clients who are undecided about mediumship and have a wonderful time watching them warm up as they identify loved ones in Heaven.

While writing this section of the book I conducted a message circle in a nearby town for a group of ten men and women who worked together. The moment I sat down I could see that one young woman named Veronica was quite uncomfortable; she seemed almost giddy. I introduced myself, talked about how I work, and then asked if anyone was nervous about the proceedings. All except for Veronica were excited to get started, so I began.

Right away I connected with a man in spirit who was standing in front of Veronica.

"Do you know the name Fred?" I asked her.

"No," said Veronica. I reminded the group that I don't hear names, so the spirit has to show me the face of a person I know in order to indicate his name.

"A name like Fred – not Frederick. A nickname, something like Fred?" I asked.

"No," she said again. Veronica wasn't making eye contact with me and was rejecting what I said with a dismissive wave of her hand. Thinking she might be anxious, I communicated with her gently, hoping to coax her to relax.

"He shows me the state of Florida, does this mean anything to you? He may be talking about himself or talking about you."

"No."

"He also shows me Ernest Hemingway, and a connection between the two of you. You're both writers."

Nothing from Veronica. I left Fred in spirit for the moment and brought other spirits through for the rest of the group, continually returning to Veronica with additional information for her to validate. *Cuba. Dad. Smoking cigars. Tall and handsome like a movie star.* I received a dismissive wave of the hand each time, and by now, about an hour into the message circle, the rest of the group was becoming just as frustrated as I. It seemed that Veronica truly did not want to be there, and I was getting exasperated by her refusal to engage even the slightest bit. Her rude manner could no longer be mistaken for nervousness.

One last time, please, Fred, I asked the spirit man.

"He shows me a shiny car key, so I know he's talking about new cars or buying cars. Did you just buy a car?"

"No," huffed Veronica once again.

"Oh, come on!" cried Susan, the guest sitting right next to her.

I opened my eyes and looked at Susan.

"Veronica, your father's name is Manfred, he owned a car dealership in Miami, and you're both writers!" said Susan. "He smoked cigars, everyone said he looked like Clark Gable, and he made regular trips to Cuba when he was younger!"

"Well, *I* didn't just buy a car!" retorted Veronica.

I thought the group was going to bodily remove her for wasting everyone's time and money. I let Veronica know that she was welcome to stay in the circle, but as she clearly did not want to participate I wasn't going to bring any other spirit people through for her.

Veronica was not open to spirit communication at all, but despite her rejection of me, the process, and the evidence offered by a spirit, her father came in first and persisted for more than an hour.

Q: "I came here with all these things on my mind that I thought my loved one would say, and she didn't. Why didn't she say the things I had in my mind that I expected her to say? I would have loved her to come through and say, 'You've had a rough couple of years, you're doing better now.'"

A: People often say to me, "How do I know you're not just reading my mind?" If a client comes with a number of things he specifically wants to hear, the spirit people for my sake may tell me, "Say this instead." That way I know, and the client knows, that I'm not just reading his thoughts. This is communication from a person in the afterlife.

Additionally, a spirit may not say what the client expects because she has something more valuable to impart. In my experience spirit people have limited connection time and will use it as efficiently as possible. You might think it's important to hear a certain message, but your loved one may feel it's more important to deliver a different one.

Q: "Can you say to a spirit person, this guest wants to talk to you, please step forward?"

A: That depends on the spirit. I can no more compel a spirit person to act than I can a physical person. And remember, a spirit may not be able to communicate with me directly or fluently. I can't control their communication abilities any more than I can insist a French-speaking person start conversing in English. They're sovereign beings, the spirit people. They're not ghosts or energies we can command to do our bidding.

That being said, your loved ones are almost always aware that you are participating in a reading and make every effort to be identified and understood. They *want* you to know that they can hear you, and if a guest asks me to call a loved one that spirit will usually find a way to get through. If the spirit has already been acknowledged earlier in a reading, it's easy enough to call him back if the guest has more questions.

Q: "How often can people come for a reading?"

A: If someone is coming for a psychic reading, for information about her future, I recommend waiting at least six months. You have to let time pass so you can see how the future is developing. With mediumship, I don't think those guidelines apply. I've had clients who come more frequently, though after a while their spirit people say, "Why are you still here? I don't have anything else to tell you. Get on with your life!"

There is no magic formula for spirit communication, and I think most mediums would agree with me. Your dad may come through brilliantly today, but not tomorrow. I may be able to connect you with your childhood sweetheart, but another medium may not. If a guest in a large group gets a wonderful but brief communication from a loved one, she might call me for an individual reading a week later. Many one-on-one clients are so excited about their experience, they'll get a group of friends or family members together right away for a message circle.

All mediums have their own personal style. It's best to ask how often he or she recommends you return.

Q: "Did you ever wish that you didn't have this ability?"

A: No, because then I wouldn't be able to pay my mortgage! The fact is, I'm blessed to have the ability to make a living doing work I love.

ABOUT THE AUTHOR

Priscilla Keresey is recognized throughout the country as one of the most accurate, compassionate, and sought-after psychic mediums. In addition to bringing the physical and spiritual worlds together for individuals and groups, Priscilla coordinates local psychic fairs, appears on radio and television programs, and acts as guest minister and medium for local Spiritualist churches. She is a keynote speaker at conferences on the topics of Creating Success & Prosperity, Reclaiming Your Connection to the Divine, and Using The Power of Your Inner Mind. She teaches workshops on developing psychic ability and offers training for mediums in her message circles.

Priscilla is also certified by the National Guild of Hypnotists as an Advanced Clinical Hypnotist, specializing in Past Life Regression, and she is an ordained Minister of Peace. She has created and taught a highly-effective six-week program on empowerment for female inmates in the New York State Correctional System.

Priscilla is the author of *It Will All Make Sense When You're Dead, Messages From Our Loved Ones In The Spirit World.* She also wrote the popular Live & Learn Guides™ series, and is the author and producer of Live & Learn Guides™ self-hypnosis audio files. She lives in New York.

To contact Priscilla, use one of the following methods:

Online	Address
www.apracticalpsychic.com	P.O. Box 226
www.liveandlearnguides.com	Putnam Valley, NY 10579
www.viahypnosis.com	
	Telephone
Facebook.com/APracticalPsychic	(914) 672-9741

ALSO BY PRISCILLA KERESEY

It Will All Make Sense When You're Dead
Messages From Our Loved Ones In The Spirit World

Psychic Medium Priscilla Keresey delivers stories, connections, and messages of hope and reunion in this light-hearted, personal book. After a brief tale of her own introduction to the paranormal, the author shares funny, poignant, and insightful words straight from the spirit people themselves. Together, the living and the dead seek forgiveness, solve family mysteries, find closure, settle scores, and come together for birthdays, anniversaries, and graduations. Quoting directly from her readings and séances, Priscilla reports the spirit perspective on mental illness, suicide, religion, and even the afterlife itself. For those readers interested in developing their own spirit communication skills, the last section of the book offers meditations and exercises used by the author herself, both personally and with her students.

It Will All Make Sense When You're Dead is chock-full of simple and entertaining wisdom, showing us how to live for today, with light hearts and kindness.

Ordering information can be found by clicking the "Products" link at
www.liveandlearnguides.com

AND...

The Live & Learn Guides™ Series

Mapping Your Destiny:
How to Use the Amazing Power of Intention
Do you ever wonder why some people seem to have it all? Are you
having trouble getting some traction on your dreams? The quickest,
most efficient way to define and create the life you want is by setting
intentions. In this book you'll learn:
- How to ask for what you want (set an intention)
- What not to do when you set goals or intentions
- The no-fail formula for designing the life you've always dreamed of

Getting the Money You Want, Not Just the Money You Need:
The Straight Path to Abundance
Have you read countless books on creating prosperity? Have you been
to the seminars and done the visualizations and still find yourself
struggling? Are you ready, now, to live in the relaxation and serenity
that comes with knowing your financial needs are always taken care
of? Then this is the last book you'll ever have to read! In this book
you'll learn:
- What's been holding you back
- How to release it, once and for all
- The six steps to ongoing prosperity

Unveiling Your Psychic Powers:
Never-Before-Told Secrets of a Psychic Medium
You may not know this, but you're already psychic. Everyone is!
While it's true that some individuals seem to have an effortless "gift"
of seeing the future, reading the past, or communicating with spirits,
every single one of us has the same tools and abilities. We just need to
learn how to use them, practice, and develop confidence. In this book
you'll learn how to:
- Distinguish a psychic impression from a self-generated thought
- Read other people and situations instantly and confidently
- Build confidence in your intuitive abilities with fun, easy exercises

A Radically Successful You:
Easy New Ways to Achieve Any Goal, Fast!
Are you tired of watching your co-workers get promoted while
you slog away day after day? Do you ever wonder how your friend
manages to be in the right place at the right time, all the time? Do
you compare yourself to self-starters or entrepreneurs and wonder
what they have that you don't? You are about to learn the secrets of
real success! You'll be one of the winners – guaranteed! In this book
you'll learn:
- Why you may not be succeeding right now
- How successful people deal with obstacles
- Six steps to creating and programming automatic success habits

Your Total Health Solution:
3 Ways. 7 Days. Guaranteed!
Do you have trouble turning off the chatter and relaxing, either at
your lunch break during the day or before bedtime at night? Does it
feel like it's been years since you had energy to try something new or
go after a long-held goal? Are you tired of feeling so rundown? If so,
this book offers you ways to return to total health in a shorter time
than you might have thought possible. In this book you'll learn:
- How to approach total health on three fronts simultaneously
- Easy-to-assimilate steps to take for physical health now
- What emotional health is, and how to begin experiencing it
- What mental balance is, and how you can find it
- What to do on Day 8 and beyond

Praying: Creating A Relationship With God
Did you ever wonder if prayer really works? Have you ever been
concerned that you're not doing it "right?" Are you repeating by rote
those old prayers from your childhood, wondering if it's really possible
that God hears that droning? You're not alone. In this book you'll learn:
- What makes a prayer a prayer
- How to create a prayer, and how to pray
- How to know your prayers are being heard and answered
- The benefits of praying
- Whether traditional prayers or homemade prayers are right for you

The Live & Learn Guides™ Self-Hypnosis Audio Series

Change Your Mind, Change Your Fortune
Abundance begins in the mind. Creating a mindset that says "Yes!" to prosperity is the key first step in creating a fortune. Listen to this self-hypnosis audio file and prepare your mind to naturally, intuitively, and rapidly attract riches into your life.

Creating True Success
We get what we focus on, and when we focus on success we create more. Listening to this self-hypnosis audio file allows you to realize the many ways you're already succeeding, opening the door for increased opportunities to achieve your goals.

Lose Weight, Feel Great!
Everyone knows that a healthy weight is more than calories in and calories out. With this audio file you can re-program your inner mind and direct your body to the shape and weight you desire.

Relax & Rejuvenate
Relax, de-stress, and create total health in your body and mind. Listen, relax, and rejuvenate!

Meeting Your Spirit Guides
Take a serene and confident guided journey to the realm of the Higher Mind, where you'll connect with your spirit guides. This guided meditation is 100% successful in bringing you together with your team on the other side. Don't miss this opportunity to learn how your guides communicate with you!

Discovering Your Personal ESP
Everyone has the ability to tap into their sixth sense. With this guided meditation you'll discover what your ESP feels like, and you'll be able to practice several techniques to hone your inherent abilities and develop confidence.

Re-Train Your Brain For The Life You Deserve!
You can use your mind on purpose to create the life you deserve.
Change your thinking and actually re-wire your brain to effortlessly
direct positive changes in your life.

Live & Learn Guides™ are available in printed or electronic format.
Live & Learn Guides™ self-hypnosis audio files are available in CD
or MP3 format. Ordering information can be found by clicking the
"Products" link at **www.liveandlearnguides.com**